IN REAL LIFE

IN REAL LIFE

MY JOURNEY TO A PIXELATED WORLD

JOEY GRACEFFA

with Joshua Lyon

Keywords
PRESS

ATRIA

NEW YORK   LONDON   TORONTO   SYDNEY   NEW DELHI

ATRIA PAPERBACK
An Imprint of Simon & Schuster, Inc.
1230 Avenue of the Americas
New York, NY 10020

Note to readers: Some names and identifying details of people
portrayed in this book have been changed.

First Keywords Press/**ATRIA** PAPERBACK edition May 2015

Keywords Press/**ATRIA** PAPERBACK and colophon are trademarks of
Simon & Schuster, Inc.

For information about special discounts for bulk purchases,
please contact Simon & Schuster Special Sales at 1-866-506-1949
or business@simonandschuster.com.

The Simon & Schuster Speakers Bureau can bring authors to your
live event. For more information or to book an event, contact the
Simon & Schuster Speakers Bureau at 1-866-248-3049 or visit our
website at www.simonspeakers.com.

Interior design by Paul Dippolito

Manufactured in the United States of America

10   9   8   7   6   5   4   3   2

Library of Congress Cataloging-in-Publication Data is available.

ISBN 978-1-4767-9430-3
ISBN 978-1-4767-9431-0 (ebook)

This book is dedicated to all the people who feel alone in the world, and to my loyal viewers—I never could have made it without you.

Contents

IN REAL LIFE

Introduction

Hello there, everyone! Well, I suppose it's just you! Hello there, you. Welcome to my first book. If you aren't familiar with me already, my name is Joey Graceffa. I'm twenty-four years old, and I make a living posting videos online. (Don't worry, they're the classy kind =P.) Whether you are a casual viewer or one of my devoted psychopaths, good to see ya again. Anyway, this is the story of my life so far. I get that it's kind of odd for someone my age to be writing a memoir, but I feel some responsibility to help inspire and comfort anyone out there who is facing challenges similar to those that I went through. There's a saying I like to live by: It's not about where you start but how you finish. I think it's important to take your experiences and grow from them rather than become a victim of your circumstances. Nothing productive comes from that mind-set.

While writing this book, I learned a lot more about myself, and as hard as it was to relive many moments that I wish could stay buried in my head, in the end it's therapeutic for me to release this information into the world.

I have kept a giant part of my life hidden for many reasons, and in this book I'm finally going to let it all hang out while giving you a deeper glimpse into all the crazy experiences that have gotten me to where I am today. If there is one thing I hope you and all my other readers can take away from my story, it is to know you're not alone. As much as you feel that no one in the world knows what you're going through, chances are you're wrong. (If you're an alien reading this, I'm sorry. No one here can relate to you.) But for real, I can't tell you how many times I felt so alone growing up and kept all of my feelings inside. It was not healthy. In no way am I trying to complain about my life, though. I accept that I had a different upbringing than most other people have, but it's made me into the man I am today and I wouldn't change a thing. So without further damn ado, here's everything that's happened so far "In Real Life."

Chapter 1

Josephina, the Friendless Dunce

I wish I could remember if the lead paint chips that I ate as a child were satisfying to my curious, bored one-and-a half-year-old self. Maybe they tasted so good that swallowing them was worth the torture they caused all the way through high school.

Somehow I doubt it. The way my mom tells it, we were living in an old apartment complex in my hometown of Marlborough, Massachusetts, a small city about forty-five minutes outside Boston best known for literally nothing. Well, that's not exactly true. A lot of shoes were manufactured there for soldiers during the Civil War. I also used to think that the cigarettes were named after the town, but I was wrong.

Anyway, my parents hadn't divorced yet (that fun news wouldn't come until one year later), so at the time, it was my mom, my dad, my older sister Nicole, and me living at home. We had an enclosed back porch that we used as our playroom, and I'd sit in front of the windows, doing my fat wobbly toddler thing, pushing around colored blocks and Fisher Price Little People. The paint on the sills was peeling and chipped, and since the windows were often open, the breeze would blow flakes of paint onto my toys. My mom isn't sure how many weeks I'd been ingesting the poison, but when she finally

3

walked in and found me going to town on a bunch of little white flecks, she snatched me up and rushed me to the doctor to get tested for lead poisoning.

A normal nontoxic amount of lead in a child's system is under 10 micrograms. According to my blood test, I had 59 micrograms! Math isn't my strong suit (thank you, paint chips), but I'm pretty sure that's almost SIX TIMES the recommended maximum. The doctors weren't really sure how it was going to affect me, but the big fear was that I would have brain damage. In truth, I'm lucky that I didn't end up with anything more severe than a learning disability, though that's not how it would feel while I was dealing with its repercussions for the next twenty years of my life.

From the start of preschool, I had a hard time acquiring basic skills like reading and simple math. My mother had me tested, and the results qualified me for special education classes. I didn't fully understand what that meant for the first couple of years of elementary school. At a certain point each day, I'd leave my regular class to go to another one, and I knew that it was a different sort of program, because the other students in it acted differently from the ones in my regular classes. This one—we called it SPED (special education) for short—was mostly made up of a lot of really hyper kids with ADHD (that's attention deficit hyperactivity disorder), troublemakers, and a few kids with Down syndrome. Looking back, I find it highly strange that the school just lumped everyone with learning difficulties into one class, regardless of their specific educational needs. But the material was taught much more slowly than in the regular class, and it was easier for me to understand.

Though none of us were fully aware of the reason we were together, all of us special education kids were friends. I grew especially close to a girl named Taylor who had mild ADHD. One day while playing tag during recess, I told her that she reminded me of a mouse, and she got really offended. But I'd called her that because she was small, and her pretty yellow hair reminded me of Pipsy the Mouse from my favorite video game at the time, *Diddy Kong Racing*. She quickly forgave me once I explained myself, and we started becoming friends.

While we probably had fewer challenges than the other kids in the class, we were still pretty different from our regular classmates. One day we saw a kid in the hallway who had a broken leg, and he was swinging himself around on crutches. We thought it looked cool and fun, like he was some sort of robot acrobat, so after school, we rushed over to Taylor's house, where there was a trampoline. We spent the entire rest of the day leaping as high as we could and then aiming to land at the edge so we'd fall off and break our legs and get to have crutches too. Luckily for us, her dad eventually came home and made us stop before we could do any permanent damage.

It wasn't until around third grade that I started to realize other kids at school made fun of the special education program. That was about the time that I got really good at sneaking down the hallway to get to my classes, and I thought no one knew that I went to them.

But in fifth grade, the truth came out, and that's when the bullying really began. One day, class was over and we were lined up at the door waiting for the bell to ring. A kid named Kevin suddenly called out to me. "Hey, Joey, you getting ready to go to SPED with the other retards?"

I blushed a deep red. "No. What are you even talking about?"

"Come on, everyone knows," he said. The bell rang, and we all filed out into the hallway. "Look," he said, pointing to a fellow SPED classmate who was on her way to class—a girl named Jackie with Down syndrome. "You can walk Jackie there!" Jackie looked over at me, waiting to see if I would join her.

To this day, I'm ashamed of my response. "I don't even know that girl," I said and took off in the opposite direction. I ended up hiding in an alcove under a stairwell until well after the bell rang, just to make sure no one saw me going to the wing of the school where our classes were held.

In school, most kids want nothing more than to fit in. I hated the idea that my peers thought less of me because I was considered "stupid." It was embarrassing. But, really, I was my own toughest critic. I cared so much about what other people thought that it began to influence the way I thought about myself. I began to believe that I was less of a person because I had a disability. I knew that I had to change something because of the effect SPED had on my self-esteem, but it would be years before I was able to do anything about it. For the time being, I just made sure to go out of my way to take a really complicated route to get to class, trying my hardest to keep that part of my life secret.

But it was too late. Other kids knew, and I was ostracized more and more. In the cafeteria, I usually sat with a small group of girls, and whenever I'd make my way to their table, all the boys would taunt me, calling me a girl. In fact, the girls I hung around with could be just as brutal as the boys. Sometimes, out of nowhere, they would all gang up on me and tell me to go sit somewhere else. They'd sing along to the tune of "It's Raining Men," but use the words, "It's raining guts, hallelujah! It's raining Joey's guts, amen!" The lines between the chorus were all about how my different insides and body parts would splat and explode all over the ground.

It sounds like a truly bizarre way to tease someone, I know. But it cut like a knife (much like the one from their song that freed my guts from my belly).

Although I was the girls' punching bag, sometimes they wouldn't want to deal with me at all and would just silently wave me away when I tried to sit with them. On one such humiliating day, I decided to lick my wounds by seeking out a frozen treat. The cafeteria had recently gotten an ice-cream vending machine, and it was considered a pretty big deal because most of the desserts you could order from the machine were pricey for the average elementary school student. After being rejected by the girls, I wanted to pretend that I was above them, so I haughtily marched up to the machine like I was the richest kid in school. I used the sixty cents I'd scrounged out of the bottom of my bag earlier that day to buy the cheapest item available—a cherry Popsicle. I turned to face the cafeteria as if I didn't have a care in the world, proudly unwrapped it, and took my first lick. My tongue immediately froze to it, just like that scene from A Christmas Story when the kid licks the flagpole.

I tried to remove my tongue discreetly at first while pretending to enjoy the Popsicle. I wiggled the bastard around in little circles, but it wouldn't budge and started to burn my tongue badly. I turned to face the wall and tugged on it hard, all the while keeping a side eye on the cafeteria to make sure no one saw what was happening. Too late. I heard someone start to laugh hysterically, and I slowly turned around to face the crowd, where everyone suddenly exploded with laughter and pointed at me. By the time a teacher finally came over to lead me away to the nurse's office so she could pour warm water over my tongue, I wanted to die.

The girls laughed the loudest at me that day, but while they could be terrible, I still tried to hang out with them because they seemed like a safer alternative than the boys. I was already becoming sensitive about people reacting to the way I behaved. I understood that I acted in a way that was considered feminine, but I didn't know how else to act. It was simply who I was. I'd been teased about it my whole life, especially by my cousins, who would call me Josephina every time they caught me trying on girls' dress-up clothes and playing with dolls when I'd visit their house. As much as I hated the nickname, I couldn't help it. I didn't want to play with those lame building blocks and plastic cars. Girl toys were much more fun.

My dad couldn't stand my disinterest in traditionally male activities, and would buy me things like basketballs or Wiffle Ball Bats for my birthday. He was always trying to forbid me from hanging out with girls and sometimes even sneered and said that I sounded gay when I talked. He pestered me to play sports my entire life, but they never interested me at all. I was terrified of getting hit in the face and breaking my nose.

But one day I watched a girls' soccer game after school with Taylor, and the players made it look like fun. It was just a lot of running around and kicking, which I felt that I could handle. I remember that I was riding in my dad's car when I told him that I wanted to join a soccer team, and I swear he almost drove off the road with excitement.

He signed me up for a team that wasn't officially affiliated with our school, so I was playing with a bunch of kids I didn't know. I was awful, but no one teased me about it to my face. The next season my dad ended up coaching, and even though I was still a terrible player, I felt safe because I knew no one would dare make fun of me with him there. Plus, my dad was really supportive and always cheered me on, even when I was making rookie mistakes like accidentally kicking the ball toward our own goal net instead of the opposing team's. Oopsie.

Our goalie wasn't exactly nice to me, but he wasn't mean either, which made him a buddy in my mind. He was a short, chubby blond kid named Alex and the only other kid on the team who went to the same school as me. He was a band geek who played the trumpet—not one of the popular kids—so I never felt intimidated by him, even though we didn't really talk much when we were at school. But he would usually at least say hi to me, which is more than I could say for most of the other kids.

One day during gym class, all the boys were separated from the girls for a game, and a bunch of the cool guys started to gang up on me. Michael, tall and broad shouldered, led the pack.

"You have no friends, you loser," he said.

"I do too!" was my big, brave, and totally unconvincing response.

"Yeah?" he sneered. "Name one."

Alex was in our class, and I pointed at him. "Alex is my friend!" Okay, maybe we weren't close, but it seemed like a safe enough bet.

"No, I'm not!" he yelled, looking mortified that I'd called him out. All the boys went *Oooooooooh* and pointed at me and laughed.

"Burn!" Michael said, cackling.

Alex and I never talked at practice after that, and my reputation as a friendless loser was officially cemented. I might as well have worn a name tag that said as much. But it was really hammered home one day in health class when we learned how to do CPR. Everyone was supposed to partner up with someone else to learn the technique. These forced divides were what I dreaded most in school because no one ever wanted to pair up with me. There were an odd number of kids in the class, and as usual I was left standing alone.

"Okay," the teacher said. "One of you will have to be a group of three. Who wants Joey in their group?"

Not a single kid raised a hand. Some of them coughed and looked away; others snickered right in my face. I remember looking out at all of them and thinking, *Not a single person here wants to learn how to save me if I was dying. LITERALLY DYING*—not even the girls who sometimes let me sit with them at lunch (although that was probably to be expected since they already took such pleasure in imagining my death). The teacher must have quickly realized how humiliating the situation was for me, and she forced two kids to let me join them. They were *not* happy about it, let me tell you.

I knew that my perceived femininity was one reason that kids didn't like me. Still, I mostly equated my unpopularity to the fact that I was in special ed. But in sixth grade, my SPED teacher, Ms. Diesel, started noticing that I was doing better than everyone else on my assignments. She began to spend extra time with me, helping me figure out math and reading comprehension problems. Toward the end of the year, she took me into the seventh-grade English teacher's class and had me read out loud for her. She thought I did a great job, so I took a math placement test and aced that too. The school decided that I was proficient enough to join all of the regular classes, and I *finally* started to feel that I was normal.

How to Deal with Bullies

There have probably been millions of words written about the best way to deal with bullies, but I don't think there is any one right answer. Every situation is different. Someone calling you a loser in the cafeteria is different from, say, getting the crap beaten out of you after school. I think that the thing to do is use your best judgment. If you can throw a clever insult right back, then by all means do it—as long as you don't think it's going to cause more damage down the road. Most bullies are cowards and are acting out from their own insecurities. A good example is guys who call other kids a "fag." The most homophobic dudes at school are probably just freaked out because they had a hot dream about their best friend and have no clue that it's totally normal human behavior to experience a little bisexuality from time to time. If you feel that you are in physical danger, then be sure to tell a parent or teacher, but if not, then there's something to be said for learning how to stick up for yourself and letting lame name-calling roll off your back. In the end, it will just make you a stronger person and better prepared for the real world because, trust me, there are a lot of grown-up bullies out there too.

Be Friends with the SPED Kids!

And not just SPED kids, but anyone in your school who is physically or mentally different. By ignoring them, you're denying yourself a chance to make a new friend. You're also missing out on an opportunity to see the world through someone else's eyes, which is a cool thing to experience. Even something as simple as saying "hi" or giving someone a high five in the hallway can make a person feel special or important. Often you need to be the one to make the first move, because the person might be too shy or intimidated to reach out. Don't be scared. You won't regret it. And besides, what have you got to lose?

Chapter 2

My Hero

I've always worshiped my older sister, Nicole. She's one of my closest friends in the world, but it hasn't always been that way. Before I was born, she was the only child—the golden-haired daughter who was used to getting all of the attention. Then I came along, and suddenly she had to compete for affection.

There's an old family story that my dad likes to tell. Neither of us remembers the incident, so who knows if it's true, but supposedly when I was a year old and she was six, she was pushing me on one of those baby-proof swings, and she unlatched it and pushed me so hard that I flew right off. I wasn't seriously injured, but it wasn't exactly a great start to our friendship.

As I got a little older and became more of a person (rather than an endless series of dirty diapers), she still didn't like me very much, but I was obsessed with her. I thought she was the coolest, prettiest, most stylish, and smartest girl in the world, and I was crushed whenever she acted mean or decided that she didn't have time for me.

Still, for a stretch of years, we were both old enough to play the same sorts of imaginary games. When I was five and Nicole was ten, we both became infatuated with the movie *A Little Princess*, which is based on a book about a little girl trapped at a boarding school with a cruel headmistress. We made up a game that we called Miss Minchin, after the villain in the story. The entire game consisted of our locking ourselves in the bathroom and pretending that Miss Minchin was forcing us to scrub it from top to bottom. I'm not sure why we thought that was fun, but my mom definitely approved of it. What can I say? We were weirdos. But I was happy just being on Nicole's radar for however long the game lasted.

We shared a bedroom for years, and I'd often wake up from a nightmare, tiptoe over to her bed, and crawl in with her. One night, she woke up as I was trying to scurry under her covers. She sat up.

"What are you doing?"

"I'm scared," I said. "Can I sleep with you?"

"What are you scared of?"

"The dark."

I heard her sigh. "You need to get over that," she said. "It's stupid. Go to the bathroom. Then you can sleep with me."

For some reason I took this to mean that she wanted me to go and stand in the bathroom with the lights out in order to face my fear of the dark. So I did. I stood there, shadows moving around me, convinced that a big hairy monster was hiding behind the shower curtain. I closed my eyes and counted to one hundred before scooting back to our bedroom as fast as I could.

"Okay," I said, tapping her on the shoulder. "I'm back."

"Did you pee?" she asked.

"No, I didn't have to," I said, confused.

"Fine, you can still sleep with me, but you'd better not wet the bed."

It was only then I realized she couldn't care less about me facing my fears. She just wanted to make sure she woke up with dry sheets. But she'd unknowingly done me a favor. Standing there in the dark that night, I may have been terrified, but I had made myself stay in there, knowing that I would be rewarded if I did. The experience taught me that if I could keep my wits together through the scary moments in life, things would usually turn out just fine. I went to sleep that night feeling stronger and more confident, relaxed by the sense that everything would be just fine. And then I peed the bed. (Just kidding!)

We moved around a lot when I was little. In fact, we never stayed in the same place for more than two years, a pattern that oddly (or not) has remained true throughout my entire life so far. My mother shared joint custody with my dad after the divorce when I was two years old, so Nicole and I spent every other weekend at his house. Dad was a ladies' man with a groovy seventies moustache. He was popular in town, and every few months he'd land a new girlfriend. Nicole and I grew really close to each one, so we were always bummed out to arrive and find a pretty stranger sitting in the living room, smiling nervously at the prospect of meeting us. But we'd get over the disappointment fast, knowing that we were about to make a new friend.

At Dad's house, Nicole and I shared a bed with him when we were younger. My sleeping arrangements at Mom's weren't ideal either. She didn't make a lot of money as a hairdresser at the local salon, and in one of the apartments that we lived in with her, I didn't even have a bed—just a mattress on the floor. I felt insecure about it, because every kid I knew had an actual bed to sleep in. Nicole knew how I felt, so one day she gathered a bunch of bins and chests from all the different rooms and put them under the mattress to lift it off the floor, creating the illusion of an actual bed frame. I was so grateful, even if it was a little wobbly.

Because of our financial issues, toys were scarce. One year for Christmas, our mom even had to take us to the local church to get presents and food for dinner. There weren't many donations, and we each went home with a second-hand jacket. This lack of toys meant that Nicole and I had to keep relying heavily on our imaginations for fun. When we visited our father, we spent hours in the woods behind his house, exploring what all the neighborhood kids called the "murder barn," an abandoned house where someone had supposedly been killed years and years before. It was creepy—pretty much what you'd expect from a place called the freaking *murder barn*—and the walls were practically crumbling. We made up stupid dares, like challenging each other to see who could spend the longest amount of time inside alone, and we always made friendly conversation with the spiders running everywhere, so they would become our buddies and not bite us. Then we'd creep through the forest together like little wood nymphs, pretending that we were on safari and on the hunt for lions and tigers. Our father, a carpenter, always had huge sheets of plywood and metal that we'd drag into the woods and use to build little forts for our games of house.

Nicole could get bossy though, and really mean out of nowhere. One minute we'd be happily pretending to be a mother and son living alone in a forest, and the next second she'd be screaming at me for saying the wrong thing and screwing up the game.

She'd also try and get me in trouble sometimes. I remember one day when we were playing in our room and out of nowhere she goes, "Come on, Joey, say *fuck*."

I told her, "No way. That's a bad word," but she persisted: "It's okay. It's just us here alone. Trust me, it's funny!"

Of course I trusted her. She was my super-awesome big sister, and so I timidly whispered the word.

"MOM!" Nicole immediately screamed. "Joey's swearing!"

Mom burst into the room. "What's going on here?"

"Joey said the F-word."

"No I didn't," I stammered. "I said . . . um . . . fire truck." But it was too late.

"Stay right there, young man," Mom said and marched off to the kitchen while Nicole smirked devilishly from her bed. Mom reappeared with a bottle of Tabasco sauce. "Stick out your tongue."

"No," I wailed. "That stuff burns!"

"Yes it does, and it serves you right. Now stick out your tongue."

I closed my eyes and did what she said, crying out as I felt the taste spread like a fire in my mouth. When Mom left the room, I started bawling with my head buried under my pillows.

"Joey?" I heard Nicole whisper.

"Go away!"

"Here, this will help." She rolled me over gently and handed me a glass of water. I took a sip and felt cool relief. "I'm so sorry," she said. "I feel awful."

And so I forgave her, as I always did, because for the most part, we were a team. I wouldn't tell on her if I caught her doing things like sneaking out of the house to play when she was grounded, and in exchange I got to hang out with her and her friends when they came over. But she did have a temper and could randomly even become violent. One day when I was in the third grade, she shoved me down the stairs, totally unprovoked. It was terrifying, and I howled with fear and pain as I hit the floor. I remember looking up and seeing her at the top of the stairs, an expression of horror on her face, as if she couldn't actually believe what she had just done. Our stepfather went ballistic, threatening to send her away to a juvenile detention center.

From then on, Nicole never physically harmed me in any way, but she still bossed me around or, worse, outright ignored me. When she was yelling at me, it meant I was in her sphere of consciousness, so I knew that I mattered. The silent treatment really sucked because I thought it meant that she didn't even care enough about me to bother yelling. The more she pushed me away, the more I wanted to be close to her. All I wanted was her acceptance.

I had another ally in the house, though: my stepfather, Bob. My mom married him when I was in first grade. He's a computer engineer and has always been kind to Nicole and me. When he first started coming around the house, I called him the Chinese man because he always brought us Chinese food. And a few years later, he brought something even better into the house: my dog. The reason we got a pet was that Bob was convinced that we needed a guard dog after his wallet went missing (never mind that it turned out he'd just left it by the grill out back). We went to a pet store at the mall (this was way before I understood the importance of rescuing dogs from shelters), and he let me choose an Australian shepherd with different shades of brown fur, like Reese's Peanut Butter Cup ice cream. I named her Bailey, and she became my constant companion. I would tie her leash to my little Razor scooter and she would pull me through the neighborhood. We played a game where I'd build little forts around myself with cardboard boxes and no entrance, and she'd then tear down the walls, tail wagging furiously, to be by my side. She slept with me every night and licked my face whenever I was feeling sad.

I really loved Bob (and still do!), not just for bringing Bailey into my life but for the attention and affection he showered on me. He moved us from the janky apartment we were living in to a big white house with a huge yard and a trampoline. It was perfect, like something straight out of a feel-good family TV show. Bob took us on vacations too, to places like Disney World and the Caribbean. He cared about all of us deeply. But when Nicole became a teenager, she fought with him and my mother constantly, the way most teenagers do. Her arguments with my mother got so bad that she ended up moving out of our house and in with my dad when I was in the eighth grade. Whenever I saw her at my dad's house every other weekend, she always had the best clothes, listened to the coolest music, and had tons of friends around. I was jealous, because, of course, my own social life was seriously lacking.

The year I started high school is when everything really changed with Nicole and me. She was a senior that year, so my parents arranged for her to come and pick me up every morning to drive me to school. On the first day, she screeched to a stop in front of my mom's house and I ran out to meet her.

"Here you go," she said, handing me a toasted bagel with cream cheese and some orange juice. She turned up her stereo and blasted techno music the whole way to school while I munched on my breakfast. When we cruised into the parking lot together, everyone stared, and I felt like the coolest kid alive. She even walked me to my first class. I didn't have a single friend, though, and when lunchtime came, I entered the cafeteria and nervously surveyed the crowd. It was like a high school movie cliché: every table was filled with different cliques. Jocks, nerds, emo kids, and druggies all sat huddled together like different tribes. I didn't fit in anywhere, and there weren't even any available seats. I cautiously approached a table of Hispanic girls, hoping they'd squeeze over to make room for me, but they just looked at me as if I was a crazy person when I asked if I could sit with them. Just then, one of my sister's friends, Ashley, walked by, and I asked her if she'd seen Nicole anywhere.

"Yeah, she's way over there in the back," she said. I craned my neck and saw Nicole and all of her popular, beautiful friends waving me toward them. I felt that all eyes were on me as I, a lowly eighth grader, crossed the cafeteria to sit with the most gorgeous group of girls in school. I adored Nicole at that moment. She could easily have ignored me, the way so many siblings do when they attend the same school. But she reached out and made my first day shine. For the rest of the year, she picked me up every morning and had breakfast waiting for me in the car. Her friends all adopted me as their pet little brother and always said hi in the hallway. I think their protection really helped me avoid a lot of bullying that first year—at least when they were around. I did get bullied in the gym locker room by upperclassmen. Before school started, I was terrified of the idea of having to shower with other people. That never ended up happening because it wasn't required, but even when I was fully clothed, the upperclassmen took turns picking on me. Sometimes it was because my clothes reeked of my mother's cigarette smoke (DISGUSTING—don't ever smoke, please!), or sometimes they'd laugh about my hair, which, now that I think about it, they had every right to considering I bleached my bangs blond. (So nineties!) But it wasn't just the bleached tips: I used gel to make my bangs stick up straight into the air. They'd ask what I used to achieve that effect, but faster than I could say, "Paul Mitchell Sculpting Gel," they'd call me a fag and say it was probably semen from another guy. I guess they'd watched *There's Something about Mary* a few too many times, but I was so clueless at the time that I didn't even really know what the word *semen* meant. I'd just laugh it off, even though I could tell from their undertone that it wasn't meant to be funny.

Even my sister was teased by her guy friends about how feminine I looked and acted. They always asked her if I was gay. She would stick up for me and tell them I wasn't, but one day she took me aside at school and told me I should start walking around with more boys because people were starting to talk. I didn't have any guy friends, though, so from then on, I began to feel extremely self-conscious about the people I was seen with. Sometimes I'd lurk behind a big group of guys I didn't know while walking down the hall just to make it seem that I was part of their gang. High school can be a scary place and I wanted to make sure I was protected (I felt like one of those tiny fishes that stick close to the side of a big shark).

It wasn't just the kids at school who were wondering if I was gay, though. One day after school, I walked into the kitchen to find Nicole and my mom sitting at the table. Mom asked me to sit down with them. Apparently Nicole had told her that I was being teased at school, and Mom straight out asked me: "Joey, are you gay?"

It was clear from the tone of her voice that there would be no judgments, no matter what the answer. She wasn't being confrontational at all, just gently supportive.

"No," I scoffed. "Of course not. I like girls."

The two of them exchanged glances as I got up and went to my room, and the subject wasn't brought up again.

As I grew older, Nicole always supported me in every decision I made, especially when it came to following my YouTube dreams. Today she lives in Boston, and we see each other a few times a year. We talk on the phone constantly. She's one of my biggest cheerleaders, and I don't think I'd be where I am today if she hadn't had my back. I love you, Nicole, even if you did push me down the stairs like a homicidal maniac.

Ten Reasons to Be Friends with Your Sibling(s)

1. You never know when you'll need someone to bring you toilet paper.

2. They will cover for you if you break something.

3. They will help you come up with an alibi if you break curfew.

4. You get a lifetime of inside jokes that no one else will understand.

5. They can help you break into new social circles at school.

6. You can trust them way more than your friends to be honest with you about your creative work.

7. They provide entertainment when you get stuck at boring relatives' houses.

8. No one else will ever understand just how crazy your parents actually are.

9. Once you're both adults, they will always have your back, no matter what happens.

10. There's a chance you will need a kidney donor someday.

A Few More Weird Games I Used to Play with Nicole

Courthouse: I would pretend to be a judge and my sister would plead different cases in front of me. I loved using my mom's wooden meat mallet as a gavel!

Manhunt: This is basically hide-and-seek with our cousins, but everyone who gets found joins the seeker and it becomes a big mob tracking you down, so it's much scarier.

Runaway orphans: Nicole and I would pretend our parents were dead, and to avoid being placed in a foster home, we'd pack up tote bags full of snacks and bottles of water and go off to live on our own in the woods.

And, last but not least: **OMG THE FLOOR IS LAVA!!!**

How to Approach Strangers in the Cafeteria

Don't freak out if you don't have a place to sit. Approach a table and ask if anyone is sitting at an empty seat. If you get rejected, move on and try again. Don't get discouraged if people are rude. Just keep trying, and no matter what, don't be afraid to sit by yourself. It can actually help cultivate an air of intrigue! People will think you're the brooding, mysterious type. The main goal here is to not end up eating alone in a toilet stall. If all else fails, sit with the SPED kids. They will always welcome you!

Why Your Own Imagination Is Better Than Your iPad

Playing inside your brain lets you develop your creative mind and manufacture fun out of thin air. Plus, your imagination is never going to run out of battery power. If there's some sort of energy apocalypse, you won't ever get bored.

Chapter 3

Warrior Mother

The first word that comes to mind when I think of my mother is *warrior*. My earliest memories of her are as a struggling single mom, working long hours cutting hair at a local salon, while still always being there for Nicole and me. Mom was the one who taught us to use our imaginations to have fun instead of relying on expensive toys, and it was Mom who taught me how to be a storyteller.

I have many memories of her being the most caring and loving person in the world, and she could always make me laugh. I loved dancing with her most. She would blast songs by her favorite band, Journey, and throw me up on her hip and boogie around the room. She also knew how much of a sweet tooth my sister and I had, so each night, she would make us frappes (scoops of ice cream, milk poured on top, and then it's all mashed up with a spoon) in our favorite cups—plastic beach souvenir tumblers with sand and seashells encased in their clear plastic bottoms.

Mom's number-one priority was taking care of us, and she did a ton with what little she had. She made sure we were happy and loved. She might ground me for a week but later that same day would come into my room and tell me that I could go hang out with my friends after all. (My dad was strict and very quick to punish me if I did something wrong.) She was the best mom in the world!

One of my favorite activities with her was going grocery shopping. We had our little routine down pat: first, we stopped by the dairy section where she'd grab me a free sample of cheese. Then she'd send me off on little errands like picking out the cereal, and on my way back to her, I'd visit the flower section and charm the florist into giving me a single rose. I'd then sneak a cookie from the bakery and surprise her with both of them as a gift. But more often than not, we'd finally get to the checkout counter only to have my mother's credit card get declined. She'd laugh nervously and ask them to run it again, making up some excuse like that she'd just made a payment. The truth was that we were broke. I don't think there's anything more embarrassing than leaving a store empty-handed after an hour of shopping. I hated that feeling.

Although she couldn't balance her bank statements, my mom always wanted to appear to be an expert on everything. If she didn't know the answer to something, she'd make one up with such enthusiastic conviction that we'd have to pretend that she was right, even when we knew she was wrong. She insisted on calling veins *ventricles* and once launched into a totally incomprehensible response when I asked her what made a car run: "The centrifugal hits the equilibrium of the motorized mechanisms . . ."

"I'll just ask Dad," I said quickly before she could say anything more. Her confidence was adorable, though, and I loved her for at least trying to answer questions that we asked even if I knew she was basically making it all up as she went along.

• • •

When I was eleven, my cousins and I went through a phase of pretending we were a family of witches, and one of our favorite pastimes was mixing special potions with all of my mom's shampoos, lotions, perfume, and hair gels. We'd pour as many different kinds of liquids that we could find into little glass jars, stir all of the ingredients together, and then study them like mad scientists over the next several days to see what would happen. The mixtures would usually separate into beautiful, cloudy layers of gunk that looked like the swirling atmosphere of an alien planet.

One day we realized we'd used up all of my glass bottles but still wanted to keep mixing. I noticed a container of hydrogen peroxide in Mom's bathroom cabinet and decided it would work perfectly. I emptied it out and filled it with liquid soap, shampoo, bathroom cleaner, body lotion, and a dash of cologne. A perfect recipe, I thought. I put it back on the shelf and forgot all about it until later that night, when I heard screams coming from the bathroom.

Uh-oh. What I didn't realize was that my mom used hydrogen peroxide as a mouthwash (go figure!), and she'd just taken a giant swish of my nasty concoction before spitting it out all over the sink. She was furious at first, but ended up laughing about it before long—which was pretty cool of her given that she could have become sick if she'd swallowed the mixture. Little did I know that she was already starting to become sick from an entirely different kind of potion—one that made the beacon of light inside of her (the one that always made me feel protected) start to fade.

• • •

When I was in about sixth grade, my mom's disease started interfering with our lives. It's possible it had been going on longer, but if it was, I didn't start noticing it until the end of elementary school. I remember seeing her with a glass of wine once or twice at the salon, but I never noticed anything drastically different about her personality when she drank.

It's odd that she began drinking heavily when she did. It would be one thing if our lives had been really rough at the time, but everything was great. She and my stepfather, Bob, were totally in love, and she was finally pulling in good money working at her own salon out of our house. I think it might have had something to do with the fact that she wasn't used to having a good life. I didn't know much about her parents. She didn't talk about them a lot, but what little I did know sounded truly awful. Her mother had died when she was little and then her father abandoned her and her six siblings. They were split up into different foster homes, and my mom ended up with guardians who emotionally abused her. In a way, I can understand how all her newly found happiness must have felt foreign compared to her childhood and what she was used to. Change, even the good kind, can be scary for some people.

My babysitter at the time had a daughter named Jonica who went to a different school than I did, and we became close friends. Even when her mom wasn't taking care of me, I'd persuade my mom to drive me over to Jonica's house so we could play with each other.

Jonica and I were very resourceful. We loved playing with Beanie Babies, but when we got bored with the ones we had, we needed a way to get more. Because those things were like crack! We had to have all of them! My mom set up an arrangement: Whenever we helped her clean up the salon and around the house, she would take us to the store and we would each get to pick one out. We were intense with our games—we spent a lot of time building houses for our Beanie families, and then making them have sex before killing them. It was magical.

One Friday afternoon I was playing at Jonica's after school when Mom came to pick both of us up for a sleepover at our house. Mom visited with Jonica's mom for a little while, and I remember noticing that they had a drink together before we left. It barely registered, but when it was time to go home, I climbed into the front seat and noticed a big orange plastic cup in the holder between us.

"What's in there?" I asked as she pulled out of the driveway.

"Water," she said.

When she tried to pick the container up, it slipped out of her hands and spilled all over the floor and seat. Call it a child's intuition, but I knew that whatever was in that cup wasn't water. She told me to grab some napkins out of the glove compartment and help clean the mess up.

When we got home, Mom was still holding the cup, and she seemed a little off to me, though not in any way I can describe because it was so subtle. I just got the distinct sense that my mother wasn't actually quite in the room with us.

"So what do you kids want to do tonight?" she asked.

"Can we set up a cushion bed in the living room?" I asked. "And watch *Halloween Town*?"

"Suuuure," she said, smiling widely. "Sounds fun!"

Her voice sounded different though, sort of high-pitched and amped up. Again, it wasn't something I could pinpoint. I was embarrassed but also a little scared. It was like an absence of the person I knew, even though she wasn't exactly acting all that different. I can't remember how or where I'd learned that grown-ups get drunk—probably from television—but I was

pretty sure that was what was going on. I didn't even really understand what "drunk" meant, except that it wasn't a good thing.

"Why don't you go set up the cushions in the living room
and I'll get you some snacks." She disappeared into the kitchen
and I could hear her slamming drawers and knocking things
around. I peeked in on her and watched as she swayed slightly
while trying to put some cookies on a plate.

"Are you okay, Mom?" I asked.

"I'm fiiiiiine," she answered with a slight slur and a funny
little smile on her face. "I'll be there in a sec, and we'll all watch
the movie together."

"No!" I yelled. I was becoming angry and confused. I didn't
know who this woman was. She looked like my mom, but
she didn't talk like her, and I didn't want to be anywhere near
her. I ran out of the kitchen and up into my bedroom, where I
slammed the door as hard as I could. I threw myself down on
the bed and started to cry. She knocked on my door.

"Joey," she called. "Come on out! Come watch the movie!"

"Go away!" I screamed.

I heard her walk away, and then stayed in my room for another ten minutes, fuming, until it occurred to me that I'd left
poor Jonica alone with her. I jumped up and ran back downstairs, where I found the two of them sitting on a pile of cushions on the living room floor.

"Come on," Mom said, patting the seat next to her. "The
movie is just about to start."

"You can't watch it with us," I said, not moving from the
doorway.

She stared at me for a few seconds before pushing herself
to her feet. "Fine," she said, looking hurt. A few moments later I
heard her bedroom door close.

I couldn't concentrate on the movie at all. I felt terrible for telling my mom that she couldn't hang out with us. Maybe she had just been acting goofy, and I was being overly sensitive.

"I'll be right back," I whispered to Jonica and tiptoed up the stairs to Mom's bedroom, knocking softly on her door.

"What?" she said. Her voice sounded muffled, as if she was talking through a pillow.

"I'm sorry, Mom. You can come watch the movie with us."

"Forget it."

"No, really. I'm sorry."

There was silence. "Mom?"

More silence. I finally gave up and went back downstairs to finish the movie. Jonica and I fell asleep on the floor and woke to the sounds of my mom cooking breakfast for us as if nothing had happened. Back to normal.

But there was another incident not long after, when our family went to a pool party hosted by Bob's best friend who lived in a fancy section of town, in a mansion with a huge backyard. My cousin Meagan came with us, and we spent the afternoon splashing around in the pool, racing each other from one end to the other, and playing Marco Polo with a bunch of other kids. I was having a lot of fun, and it wasn't until the party was over that I noticed my mom was acting strange again. She was talking and laughing really loudly, sort of as if she was a kid herself. I knew that she was drunk. Meagan and I were still in our swimsuits, and I was shivering as I tugged on Bob's arm. "You're going to drive us home, right?" I whispered.

"Yup," he whispered. "Don't worry, kiddo."

During the ride home, Mom laughed and gossiped about different people at the party while Bob kept telling her to be nice. We got home, and everyone went to bed. I probably would have forgotten the whole thing if Meagan hadn't told her parents that my mom had gotten drunk. They flipped out, and it caused a huge rift between our families. I could still hang out with Meagan, but never at our house; I had to go to hers. It made me feel ashamed, as if our house was too dirty for guests. But it wasn't the house that was messed up. It was my mother.

Over the next year, things really began to deteriorate. One day I was sitting in the living room watching television when I heard a terrible crashing sound. I ran out of the room and saw my mother crumpled up in a ball at the bottom of the staircase. I stood there frozen and in a flash pictured the worst: a fractured spine and my mother confined to a wheelchair for the rest of her life. But she used the banister to pull herself back up and wandered into the kitchen before I even had a chance to ask her if she was all right.

To make matters worse, Mom and my stepfather split up for a while when I was twelve years old. Bob sold the big white house, the home that had been my rock. It had been the place that I'd lived at for the longest up to that point in my life. I had thought I was going to grow up there. We moved to a smaller rented ranch house, and Mom was now the only adult around, although she was hardly acting like one. By the time I entered seventh grade, Mom was drinking every night. Nicole was also aware of how rapidly things were declining, but she had such an active social life and played a lot of sports, so she wasn't around very much to see the worst of it. But whenever she was home, the two of them were almost always at each other's throats.

One day, I got off the school bus and found the house empty. I was confused, since my mom was usually home from work by then. I didn't know what to do so I just made some toast and plopped down on the living room floor to watch Nickelodeon.

About an hour later, I heard a car screech into our driveway and two doors slam. My mother and a strange blond woman came bursting in through the front door. They were both obviously tanked, but Mom was in way worse shape than the other woman.

"Joooooeeey?" she called out. "Mama's home!"

She and the woman tottered into the living room.

"There you are! This is my friend Amy!" I vaguely recognized the woman. I'd seen her a few times before down at the salon.

"Aren't you just the cutest," Amy said, and reached her hand out to tousle my hair. I ducked out of reach.

There was something different about Mom that day. By that point, I'd gotten more and more used to seeing her drunk, but now she seemed even more messed up than usual. Her eyes were bloodshot and darting around the room. She seemed incredibly on edge.

I turned off the television and went to my bedroom, slamming the door. I sat on my bed, confused and frustrated by what was happening. After about fifteen minutes, I heard Amy leave.

I left my room and saw Mom pouring herself a drink, and something inside me snapped. "Are you kidding me?" I screamed. "It's four o'clock in the afternoon!" I ran across the kitchen, snatched the vodka off the kitchen table, and tore out into the backyard. I ran as far back as I could and emptied the entire bottle. I heard my mom follow me out, but she just stood near the back door, yelling, "What are you doing?" over and over, as if she couldn't believe what she was seeing. Once the bottle was empty, I marched past her back into the house.

"The joke's on you," she said. "That was Nicole's vodka."

I didn't care if it was Nicole's. It was my mom who had been drinking it. I knew that my sister drank with her friends sometimes, but Nicole never got all weird like Mom did. I ignored her and started to go back to my room when I heard the front door slam shut.

I peeked out the window and saw Mom wandering out into the neighborhood. I was worried she was going to get hit by a car, so I decided to run after her, but before I did, I called my dad. "Please come get me," I said. "I think Mom's gone crazy."

"I'll be right there," he said. "Go into your room and wait for me."

Instead, I ran out the door just in time to see Mom disappearing behind a house a few doors down. Thankfully there weren't any cars in the driveway and it didn't look like anyone was home, so I crept along the side of the house and peered into the backyard. My mom was flat on her back, crying, and holding a big stick straight up toward the quickly darkening sky.

I walked over to her and tried to lift her to her feet.

"Come on Mom, it's time to go home," I said.

"No," she said, shaking herself free, tears still streaming down her face.

I sat down beside her and started to plead. "Mom, please. Someone is going to see you, and they might call the cops. Just come back inside with me."

"No, you're ungrateful," she said with a sniffle.

"I'm just worried," I said.

"I'm going to die."

"Don't say that. You're not going to die."

"I am. And I'm going to come back as a little blue jay."

"Mom . . ."

"No, listen. This is important. Once I die, whenever you see a blue jay, you're going to know that it is me looking after you." She waved her stick in the air again. "Just like that one."

I looked up but I didn't see any birds anywhere. A huge wave of grief washed over me. She looked sad and pathetic lying there with tears in her eyes. I tried to remember the mom from my earlier childhood, the one who was always ready to hug me if I skinned my knee, who brought me soup in bed when I was sick, who always tucked me in at night. That woman was gone, replaced with this stranger who had my mother's face. I wondered if it was my fault. Was I such a terrible son that she had to drink to escape her life? I started crying. I couldn't figure out how it had gotten to this point. Just a year ago, everything had been perfect. My family was together, and my biggest worry was making sure I got home from school in time to watch *Pokémon*. But now my mother had developed this alter ego that came out when she drank. Since Nicole was hardly ever around, I'd become the parent at just thirteen.

I heard a car door slam in the distance and my father calling my name. I got up, ran back to our place, and told him where she was.

"Wait in your room for me," he said. "Go on."

I stayed in the living room, though, and watched through the window as he went to fetch her. A few minutes passed before he appeared again with my mother half draped over his shoulder. I ran to my room before they came inside.

A few minutes later, Dad knocked on my door and came in and said, "Look, Joey, your mom is going to go away for a while." I wasn't surprised, but I was scared.

"Where is she going?" I asked.

"To a rehab center. She'll be gone for a few weeks. I already called Bob, and he's going to move in and take care of you while she's gone." This made me feel relieved. I missed Bob, and I hoped that maybe once Mom got out of rehab and everything returned to normal, they might even get back together.

She was supposed to be gone for a month. The rehab was about half an hour away, but we weren't allowed to visit for the first few days while she went through detox. After that, the doctors moved her into the main treatment center, and Bob took us to visit her every Wednesday afternoon. It was clear from the start that she hated it there.

"I don't belong in this place," she said the first time we came to visiting hours. She was wearing sweatpants and a sweatshirt, her ponytail still damp from a shower. She was sitting on the bottom bunk in a room full of bunk beds, like some sort of summer camp cabin for grown-up boozers. "Everyone in here is crazy!" The thing is, I think she was right. There were scary-looking people rocking back and forth in the hallways and mean-looking ladies with needle tracks all up and down their arms, their faces distorted from meth use. "I just got drunk a few times," Mom pleaded with us. "But these people are hard-core drug addicts!"

I felt bad for her, but Bob was adamant about her staying. "You need help. You need some time to do some work on yourself before you can come back and try to take care of Joey and Nicole."

She finally put her foot down after three weeks. No one could legally keep her in there, and she came back home. And things were great—for a while. She stayed sober for three months. It felt incredible to have my mom back. I'd missed her so much. The warm glow she carried inside her returned and made me feel happy and safe. It was also awesome to have Jonica over and not have to worry about Mom acting up. When she did start drinking again, she managed to keep it under

When I was in first grade, my mom took Nicole and me out of school early to get these professional shots taken. I remember feeling really naked and uncomfortable being shirtless under my overalls. But even then I knew I had to suck it up so the photographer could get his shot. (Hmm, I wonder if he's in prison now.)

Disney World! This was the first vacation Bob ever took our family on, back when I was in kindergarten. Nicole and I were so freaking happy to be there that she didn't fight with me once.

Me and my mom in Disney World! #model

Meet my dad, the macho man of Marlborough, Massachusetts. (Those blue eyes! The moustache!) This was taken at my grandmother's house when I was around four years old.

We used to get all dolled up for Easter Sunday. Mom and Nicole are showing off their fancy hairstyles. I'm showcasing my ability to fit four pieces of strawberry Hubba Bubba in my mouth at once. Easter baskets rule! (We were living in an apartment where I didn't have my own bed, so the little things really counted.)

Thanksgiving at my aunt's house. My family was in a really good place at this time. I also loved getting to see and play with my cousins since we were all a little weird and had crazy imaginations.

This is my childhood best friend, Jonica, back when we were both in kindergarten. Mom wanted to take a quick photo of us one day, so we grabbed props—a vase full of flowers for me, and a blue pom-pom wig for her. Nothing about this seemed weird at the time.

Josefina, in full effect! This girl was a random neighbor, and for some reason my mom thought it would be hilarious to pose me in a dress, heels, and a giant red wig left over from Halloween. Who am I kidding? It was all me!

Dad buried me in the sand during one of our annual trips with his family to Higgins Beach, Maine. After this photo was taken, he abruptly turned around and walked away, leaving me for the crabs. JK!

I landed the lead role in the eighth grade production of *Life of the Party*. I loved my braces—I could have gotten away without having them (my teeth weren't *that* bad), but today I'm so glad I did.

Brittany and I acting wild in Amanda's kitchen while microwaving some frozen pretzels.

I got my braces off in ninth grade, and my big Joey smile made its first real appearance. Also, I swear those blond streaks in my hair are natural and caused by the camera flash. Seriously!

For my ninth grade yearbook photo, I decided to wear two polo shirts on top of each other and pop both collars. The layered look was very hot back then. Or so I thought.

I went to prom with Allison, even though she had a boyfriend at the time. He was NOT happy, but whatever. I selected this white tux after seeing it on a floor display at the rental center. Hey, I know what I like when I see it!

I'm dressed as Nintendo's Kid Icarus at the 2012 Anime Expo. The costume looks pretty finished, but all I can see are the details that got left out due to my being distracted by Mike!

Meghan and I filmed a techno remix video of the *Pokémon* theme song. I rocked my classic nerd glasses. (Note that there are no actual lenses in them.)

Me, Luke, Ingrid (his girlfriend at the time) and YouTuber Fleur all ran off for a quick getaway to Catalina Island.

Rocking the red carpet at the 2012 MTV Movie Awards! I think I hid it pretty well, but I was having major anxiety about interviewing people like Victoria Justice, the cast of *Awkward*, and Jackie Emerson from *The Hunger Games*.

Here's Brittany and me at our very first VidCon. Ignore the sign—it was definitely not an FML moment. But we did have a WinterSpringPro video with that same title, so we thought it was cute!

You can tell by the awkward smile on my face that I wasn't ready for this shot. That's Luke behind me and Meghan by my side—and this is the very first photo I took with either of them! The other two are YouTubers Michael Aranda and Kristina Horner.

Just another day on the job—Meghan, Cat, and I visited this place full of trampolines for teen.com. We spent the day jumping up and down—our headaches afterward were worse than any hangover.

My Neighbor Totoro became my roommate Totoro after I bought this giant beanbag shaped like one of my favorite anime characters of all time.

When I took this selfie, I had no idea that I was going to meet Preston for the very first time just a few hours later.

Regardless of what happened between us, I'm still happy that Sam helped me decide on the green Sperrys.

I finally got rid of my emo hair! Best decision ever!

My little Squish!! Jett is six years old here, and the photo was taken when I went home for Christmas, right after filming *The Amazing Race*.

My fellow YouTubers at the 2013 VidCon! Back row, from left: Jenna Ezarik, yours truly, Marcus Butler, Tyler Oakley, Jim Chapman, Tanya Burr, Alfie Deyes. Bottom row, from left: Louise Watson, iJustine, Zoe Sugg, Louis Cole.

My high school best buds Hannah and Mariah came to visit me in LA in 2014. I love that we are still as close as we were back in the crazy weird days of our youth.

Here's an outtake from the official *Storytellers* cast photo shoot! From left: Devyn Smith, Pierson Fode, me, Kristina Cole, Jake Thomas, and Jessica Lu.

The first time that *Storytellers* ever appeared on a movie theater marquee! Such an amazing experience. Thank you to everyone who came!

control at first, and I still held out hope that maybe the worst was all behind us.

But soon she began to come home paranoid and freaked out that people were coming to get her. When I'd ask her who was after her, she couldn't say.

A good example of just how bad she'd gotten was the night my friend Zak slept over. He was the son of a friend of my mom's, and they lived three towns over, so we didn't get to see each other very often. But I was always happy when I did. He was skinny with short blond hair, and we loved to play video games together. One night he was staying over when Mom started in about how a bunch of men were coming to get her. Zak and I got so freaked out that we barricaded ourselves in my room with my dog, Bailey, and slept with butcher knives under the pillows. I had always gotten the sense that Zak didn't exactly come from the most stable household, so if he was scared too, I knew things must be pretty terrible.

I realize now that no one was coming for her and she was just being delusional. But at the time it was terrifying, and I couldn't figure out who this woman with the face of my mom was. I just wanted my old mom back.

Whenever Nicole was home, she wasn't having any of my mom's behavior. The two of them began to fight with each other over the smallest little things. If Nicole left a dirty plate in the kitchen sink, Mom would start in on her hard, but Nicole didn't take her seriously at all when she was drunk and so she'd ignore Mom, which just escalated Mom's anger until Nicole had no choice but to start screaming back at her.

My mom's drinking and all of their fighting ended up driving Nicole out of the house. She couldn't take it and moved in with my dad. I was devastated about losing Nicole. I felt abandoned, and while I entertained the thought of maybe asking if I could move in with Dad too, I couldn't bring myself to leave Mom. I cared about her too much and felt that I needed to be there to take care of her. And it was a good thing I did, because a little less than a year after my mom got out of rehab, Bob moved out again. They fought constantly and couldn't seem to make it work. So suddenly it was just my mom and me living together, and I felt more than ever that I had to be strong for her. But it was hard. All I wanted was to have a mother who could take care of me. It didn't seem like things could get any worse. Until they did.

Our year lease on the ranch house ran out, and one week while I was on vacation in Maine with my dad and his side of the family, my stepdad decided to help out by renting another apartment for my mom and me to live in. Although he was living in a new place, he still wanted to make sure we had a roof over our heads.

The vacation was amazing. My dad and I were finally getting along great after a childhood of him not really knowing what to make of me. I spent the whole time building sand castles, and Dad helped me get the courage up to ride my first roller coaster at an amusement park. The whole time I knew that I had no idea what I'd be returning to when I went home, but I tried to push the thought out of my head and enjoy myself.

It was bad enough coming home to a totally new place, but Mom and Bob did something truly unforgivable while I was away, something that I still have trouble reconciling today: they gave Bailey to an animal shelter because the apartment didn't allow dogs. I was devastated. I'd gone from living in a beautiful house with an amazing dog and having my family together. Now I'd lost my furry best friend, my sister had moved out, my mom had split up with a stepdad I adored, and I was living in the tiniest two-bedroom apartment ever with zero privacy. When I returned home from vacation to this new life, I sobbed for a solid hour, wondering how everything had gotten so bad so fast. I just didn't understand, and I felt totally alone, especially without Bailey to lick away my tears.

I was too embarrassed to show the few friends I had at the time, like Zak and Jonica, where I was living now. Aside from the incidents they'd witnessed with my mom being drunk, they had otherwise known me as this fortunate kid who had an awesome life in a great house, but now I was in a bad part of town in a sketchy apartment. I didn't know how to tell them we now had no money. I'd already gone through most of my school years feeling like less of a person than everyone else due to SPED classes and bullying, and this latest life development didn't help things at all.

Our new neighborhood was pretty run-down, and I was a little freaked out about walking to the bus stop alone. My mom was nice enough to drive me up the street to the pickup stop every morning, but she had a really old silver car with a broken muffler that was so loud it sounded like a military helicopter taking off. All the other kids walking to the bus stop would point and laugh as we drove by, so I quickly learned to shrink down in my seat as far as possible and then have Mom drop me off around the corner so that no one would see me.

That car was a nightmare on wheels. One day when I stayed home sick from school and Mom took me to Dunkin' Donuts to get a bagel, the car ran out of gas right at the drive-through window. Looking back at it now, it's so hilarious and white trash, but I was beyond mortified at the time. A bunch of employees wearing brown aprons had to come out and push our busted old vehicle out of the way and into the parking lot. Worse, I then had to walk with Mom to the gas station—still in my pajamas—to get fuel.

At the time, the only way I felt that I could escape all of my troubles was when I was playing *RuneScape*, a free online role-playing game. I could disappear into another world and pretend that I was someone else. One day I came home from school and switched on my computer as usual, with no clue that my life was about to hit an all-time low. Nobody was home, which wasn't too unusual—Mom had been working a little later than in the past at the salon. But when I came out of my computer game reverie several hours later, there were shadows on the wall. I tried my mom's cell phone, wondering if she'd stopped to get groceries, but there was no answer. I went back to my game, but I couldn't get into it. I was nervous and distracted and had the distinct feeling that something was wrong.

Suddenly the front door opened, and my mom fell into the house, calling out my name in her sing-songy drunk voice. *I should have known.* Then I heard a second voice. Amy, her drinking buddy.

"Joey, where are you?" my mom called out again, and I decided that I just couldn't deal with this anymore. I'd been happily roaming through forests with my elf friends online, and the thought of being thrust into the harsh reality of my mom's drunken antics was just too depressing. She wasn't a mean and abusive drunk, but I couldn't stand watching her become like a child who couldn't take care of herself.

On a normal day when she was drunk, she would just get very emotional and complain about everything that was wrong in her life, as if I were responsible for it. And it worked—she knew how to make me feel bad for her. But that day I wanted nothing to do with it. I quickly closed my laptop and hid under some clothes in the closet that connected our two bedrooms.

I was just in time. My mom came stumbling into my room, followed by Amy. "Joey?" Mom yelled. "JOEY? WHERE ARE YOU?"

"Shhhh," I heard Amy say. "He's probably at his dad's house."

Mom ignored her. "Joey? Joey? Where are you?" I heard her leave my room and stomp through the apartment. I pulled more clothes up over me and buried my head in my knees to try to make myself even more invisible, but something sharp was digging its way into the side of my butt. I fished out one of Mom's high heels and tossed it to the side.

I heard Amy helping my mom into her room. The bed-springs squeaked, and I could picture Amy tucking her under the covers when suddenly I heard my mom burst into tears. She wasn't just crying; she was out-and-out sobbing and taking huge gulps of air between choked wails.

I started to panic. *Was she hurt?* But I could hear Amy asking her the same thing. "Are you okay? What's wrong?" she kept repeating. So I knew there wasn't any sort of physical injury. I stayed hidden in the closet, and prayed that Mom would stop crying and fall asleep and that Amy would leave. I blamed Amy for what was happening. *Don't you know she's not supposed to drink?* I thought. *Why are you still hanging out with her and taking her to bars?*

Mom suddenly turned on Amy. "Get out of here!" she said. It was as if she had read my mind. "Get the hell out of my bedroom!"

I heard a few muffled thumps and then the sound of Amy yelping in pain. I couldn't take it anymore—I crawled out from underneath the clothes and peeked through the crack in the closet door. What I saw shocked me.

Amy was on the bed straddling my mother, who was throwing punch after punch at her. Amy managed to restrain her wrists to avoid being hit most of the times, but a few times my mom clocked her pretty hard. Amy kept trying to calm Mom down by making soothing sounds and telling her to hush, that everything was going to be okay. I was seriously freaked out—Mom was acting like Linda Blair in *The Exorcist.* I half expected her head to start spinning around and spewing vomit.

Suddenly she went completely limp. I could hear both her and Amy trying to catch their breaths, when a low moan escaped my mom's lips. She mumbled something.

"What?" Amy asked.

"I want to die," my mom said. "My life is horrible. Everything is terrible and I can't take it anymore. Just . . . just please kill me."

Amy looked as shocked as I felt. How could she say something like that? If anyone should feel that way, it was me (although I never could). It seemed so selfish of her to even think her life was that bad when everything she was doing had made my life way worse than hers.

"I want to die," Mom repeated, louder this time and somewhat calmer. "I'm not joking. Please, just kill me. I know you can do it."

"I'm not going to kill you, Debbie," Amy said. But she hadn't moved from the bed; she was still pinning my mother down.

"It would be so easy," Mom said. "Just take the pillow and put it over my face. Suffocate me. It would be fast and painless. Please, just kill me."

I couldn't believe what I was hearing. I wanted to run into

44

the bedroom and shove Amy off her. I kept thinking, *What if she does it? Am I about to watch my mother die?* I was paralyzed with fear. I couldn't move a single muscle out of terror at the thought that I might be about to watch my mother's life end. *Why am I not getting up?* I thought. *I have to stop this madness.*

"Do it!" my mom screamed.

"I'm not going to kill you, Debbie!" Amy repeated, louder this time. I felt my whole body relax and realized that I'd been holding my breath. I gulped in air and tried to get my heart to stop pounding out of my chest.

Amy climbed off my mom and sat on the side of the bed while the sobs continued. My leg began to cramp up, but I didn't want to move. I couldn't let them know that I'd just witnessed such a dark moment. My mom rolled over onto her side, crying as Amy rubbed her shoulders. After around thirty minutes, my mom started snoring softly and Amy crept out of the room. When I heard the front door close gently, I stood up and opened the closet door a bit. Part of me wanted to crawl into bed with my mom, curl up beside her, and whisper that everything was going to be okay. The other part of me wanted to tear out of the house and start running until I couldn't run any more.

That's what I did.

I let the front door slam behind me and ran as fast and as far as my legs could take me. Before I knew it, I found myself shivering on a park bench, my heart beating so hard I thought it was going to explode out of my chest. I hadn't stopped to grab a jacket, and it was already dark out. I felt better, though. I didn't ever want to go back to that house. I started fantasizing about what it must be like to have a normal family, how lucky my friends were that they didn't have to deal with this kind of stuff. I'd had a taste of a normal life once, and I prayed that someday things would return to the way they had been when I was younger.

After a while, the cold settled in. I started to get a little creeped out, sitting by myself in the dark. And although going home was the last thing in the world I wanted to do, I knew I didn't have the courage to do something drastic like run away. My version of running away had become my video games, the fantasy worlds I could disappear into as long as I kept my headphones on and my eyes focused on the screen.

I felt my stomach rumble. I was starving. Feeling defeated, I got up and slowly made my way home. The house was quiet when I got there, except for the sound of soft snoring still coming from my mom's room. I heated up some chicken nuggets and went into my room. I made sure that both of the closet doors connecting our spaces were shut tight and slipped back into my *RuneScape* game as if nothing had happened at all, my homework be damned.

At the time, I didn't tell anyone in my family what had happened. I think I was so afraid of losing my mom that I wanted to protect her. I knew that what I'd witnessed was disturbing enough that someone might take her away from me, and despite all the scary insanity she put me through, I still loved her so much.

I realize now that I should have told someone, and my advice to anyone who is going through something even vaguely similar is to call an adult. No kid deserves to go through that sort of abuse. Because that is what it is—abuse. It might not seem like that while it's happening, since it's the parent who is experiencing something crazy, but that's just the problem. The person is a PARENT. It's the parent's job to take care of the kids, and when they don't, it's abuse. You'll be helping both yourself and your caretaker if you let someone know when things are spiraling out of control.

Do You Think Your Parent Might Be an Alcoholic?

If the answer is yes, the most important thing to remember is that it is not your fault. Alcoholism is a disease, and like any other disease, it can be treated. The National Association for Children of Alcoholics has a bunch of resources on its website, nacoa.org. Check them out, and also be sure to tell an adult you trust—another family member, a teacher, a guidance counselor—what you are going through. If you feel safe with your parent, try talking to him or her about your concerns while he or she is sober. Always remember that you aren't alone, and there are people who can help you if you ask.

Chapter 4

Big Dreams and New Friends

There were a few things that kept me from going totally insane during those dark years with my mom: creating videos, acting, making some great new friends, and discovering music.

By the time I hit fourth grade, I had been begging for a camcorder for Christmas for years. Once Bob came into our lives, I finally got one. I promptly made my first movie—an exhaustingly thorough tour of our house, from the attic to our basement. (It would have been riveting footage if I'd only remembered to hit Record. :-/)

Over the next several years I made little adventure movies constantly, mostly starring my cousins and myself, because my early obsession with video wasn't just about making up and directing stories. I loved being in front of the camera too. Being able to see something I'd envisioned inside of my head suddenly come to life on a screen blew my little Joey mind.

But I wanted to do something bigger, something a larger audience than just my family would see. When I was in sixth grade, I heard that the seventh graders were putting on a production of *The Wizard of Oz*. I was determined to be a part of it but only seventh graders were allowed to audition. I went to the principal's office and begged him to let me be a part of it anyway. But he wouldn't budge, bringing out the old "If we made an exception for you we'd have to make an exception for everyone" line, one of the worst sentences in the English language.

So I kissed my dreams of the yellow brick road good-bye.

The following year's performance was of a lesser-known play (as in, no one had ever heard of it). *Dig It! A Musical Tale of Ancient Civilizations* revolved around two archaeologists who discover the bones of Lucy, a 3.2-million-year-old skeleton that comes back to life and gives a series of musical history lessons. There were no witches or flying monkeys or talking scarecrows, but I didn't care. I just wanted to be on that stage.

Kids who wanted to audition were given a copy of the script to rehearse, and I rushed home after school to study the lines with my mom. The scene was the play's opening, which basically consists of the two archaeologists in a cave exclaiming things like, "Where are we?" and, "Wow, Ethiopia is scary in the dark!"

"You've got to project your voice," my mom instructed. "Otherwise no one will be able to hear you."

At the audition the next day, I got up on stage and screamed my lines as loud as I could. I genuinely thought I'd nailed it, so I was devastated when the call sheet got posted and I saw that I'd only made it into the chorus.

But like any other good seventh-grade actor, I was determined to make myself stand out even in the smallest role. And it was a pretty small role: I had one line of my own—except that it wasn't so much a line as it was a single word. And technically it wasn't even one word. It was *spelling out* one word— Mississippi: M-I-S-S-I-S-S-I-P-P-I. It was so random, but damn if I didn't make it count. No one has ever spelled that state with more gusto, and no one ever will.

When I finally got to high school, there was a drama club

called Dessert Theater, and aside from the jocks, the kids in that group were the most popular in school. They were respected, and I was determined to become a part of them.

Dessert Theater put on three thirty-minute plays a year. There were core members of the group, but anyone in the school could audition for their productions, even little no-body eighth graders like me. But I knew I was low on the social ladder (even with all of Nicole's support), and so when I audi-tioned for their first play of the year, I didn't expect anything to happen—especially after I showed up and saw that I was the youngest person on the stage and my feet didn't even touch the ground when I sat in the chair they provided. I also forgot that I was supposed to speak to the audience and spent the en-tire audition talking directly to the guy from Dessert Theater who was running lines with the prospective actors.

When the cast was announced the following Monday, a huge crowd formed around the posted list. I tried to act casual as I strolled up, waiting until there was a space for me to move forward instead of elbowing my way to the front like everyone else. When I finally had the chance to see the list, part of me couldn't believe the sight of my name up there and felt a huge rush of relief and nervous excitement. But before I could get any closer to see what my role was, I felt a tap on my shoulder.

"Hi, Joey," a girl said. "My name is Kristen. I'm the director and just wanted to say how excited we are to work with you. We thought you were so cute and funny, and I knew we had to have you!"

I was in such a daze that I could hardly understand what she was saying. She said she'd see me at the first table read later that day, after school, and then I floated away to my next class. It wasn't until I got to the reading that I realized I'd been cast in the lead role. I was thrilled out of my mind, but also a little intimidated by how many lines I'd have to memorize.

The play was a student-written piece, "Life of the Party," and the plot was really freaky. Basically there's this little kid whose older sister is having a slumber party. He gets jealous that no one pays any attention to him, so he puts sleeping pills in their drinks and knocks them all out. He's also obsessed with a country western star, so I had to speak with a deep cowboy drawl (although I would forget and slip in and out of it constantly), wear a giant orange cowboy hat, and jump around the stage on a stick horse.

The character seemed like a budding serial killer to me, but I gave the performance my all and got great reactions from the audience.

The experience gave me the confidence to try out for the spring musical, *Anything Goes*. The problem was that my voice was changing and I sounded like a squeak toy, so I didn't make the cut. I was mortified. Dessert Theater was my escape from home life. I got to be around fun, cool kids, not stuck at home all the time with a sad, drunk mother. I desperately wanted to continue to be a part of it, and not getting in crushed me. Without a performance to rehearse, I needed both a distraction from my mom and a new creative outlet. Which is around the same time that I met a girl named Brittany Joyal.

We had in fact been in the same kindergarten class and were friends back then in that way that everyone in kindergarten is forced to be friends with each other—like, "You two are little. Play!" I recognized her when she showed up in my health class that year and the two of us were paired together by our teacher, Ms. Merritt, to do a project on addiction. Now that I think about it, maybe I can thank Ms. Merritt for my entire career, since she's the one who set us up. But the truth is that Brittany and I would have found each other in some other way regardless—especially since we shared the same totally bizarre sense of humor. Our debut performance together is a perfect example. We were assigned coffee as our addictive substance to study. It seemed like such a boring subject, and that made me want to do something extra special so it would stand out.

"I really like acting," I told Brittany during our first brainstorming session. "What if we did some sort of skit showing how bad coffee addiction can get?"

"I love acting too!" she said. "I can make myself cry on demand. Wanna see?" And suddenly right there in the middle of class, tears started streaming down her face. I knew right in that moment that this girl was insane—and that we needed to be best friends.

In retrospect, there are a lot of different ways we could have acted out how coffee can have negative effects. We could have pretended to act really hyper, like Jessie Spano in that one episode of *Saved by the Bell* where she gets addicted to caffeine pills. Or we could have pretended we were having massive, painful headaches brought on by coffee withdrawal.

Instead, I decided to play a maniac who became incredibly violent when he drank too much coffee, which of course is not actually a thing that happens, as far as I know. (If that were the case, every office in America would be a war zone!) But we also wanted to show that in moderation, coffee could be quite helpful in some situations. So we developed a scene where Brittany was inside her house drinking one cup of coffee, while I hid outside her window, guzzling tons of cups of coffee. I then climbed inside and pretended to beat her up, but she saved herself by pretending to throw her single cup of hot coffee in my face. Symbolism! Humor! Success!

Okay, I understand that the scenario seems pretty lame from the outside. But Brittany and I had lots of fun. We almost didn't make it through our skit because we were laughing so hard. The students in our class had no idea what to make of us. I think they were a little weirded out, but we got an A on the project, and after that, we were bonded for life.

Brittany and I were constantly messing around with my camcorder on weekends and after school, making up stupid skits and short films. They *might* have been considered cute if we had been in fifth or sixth grade, but by the time we were freshmen in high school, everyone around us was experimenting with dating and drugs and alcohol, while we were still playing kid games like "secret agent."

Here's a typical plot from one of our films. Brittany and I are hanging out in my attic, pretending it's our Secret Agent Headquarters. We get a call from The Chief (clearly my voice), who says that we're urgently needed in the lab. We suit up, attaching our secret agent equipment (small balloons, dead cell phones, and fake plastic laser guns) to our special secret agent belts. We rush down to the lab, which is my bedroom. You can hear my mom and stepfather—they were back together at the time—loudly chatting away in the next room about what to have for dinner, but we just ignore them and exclaim, "The Chief is missing!"

But wait—I see a clue. Someone has drawn an arrow pointing to Italy on my globe! So we rush off to Italy by getting into our flying car (A.k.a., my mom's gray Chevy Suburban; her old silver clunker had finally died by that point. Thank god.). We press a bunch of fake buttons on the dashboard and the car takes off into the air. You can tell because our bodies fly back into the seats due to the force of the liftoff (even though it's absolutely clear in the video that the car itself isn't even moving). We exit the car and are now in "Italy," which is just another area of my attic. We don't find The Chief, but we do find a rare gem (a piece of costume jewelry snagged from my mother's dresser) and for some reason decide that we need to blow the place up. The movie ends with us falling onto the grass from the force of the explosion. Cut.

I don't know what we were thinking. The whole thing made no sense, but it didn't matter. We were having a blast, and I'd found a friend and partner, someone who loved playing around in her imagination as much as I did. It was basically an anything-goes creative environment. The stuff we produced didn't necessarily have to be good; the important part was that we were having a blast and cementing a friendship that would end up launching our lives into places we didn't even dare to dream about back then.

We had another friend who sometimes appeared in our early videos, a girl named Amanda with dark hair and freckles. I'd met her in history class when I saw her putting Bugle chips on the end of each of her fingers and waving her hands around like she had claws. I cracked up and whispered that I did the same thing when I ate them, and from then on she and Brittany and I were the three amigos. She was fiercely loyal to Brittany and me and gave the best death stares to anyone who bothered us in school. Amanda was super into art and just as big a geek as us—she loved anime and video games. Brittany and I hung out with her at her house on the weekends because she had a huge living room, as well as a swimming pool that was featured prominently in many of our first minimovies.

In addition to making friends, another important early high school development was my discovery of music. In the years leading up to this point, I'd never paid much attention to it. Maybe it's because I was obsessed with video games and making my own videos—there was already so much stimulation in my life that I didn't feel like I needed anything else or that anything was missing.

But that all changed when I discovered the Veronicas.

I was hanging out at my friend Alison's house after school one day. Alison was one of the prettiest and most popular girls in school—very all-American, with blond hair, perfect skin, and big green eyes. She'd decided that she liked hanging out with me. I guess I made her laugh or something. I didn't care what the reason was; I was just happy to be at least orbiting the cool kids' group. The rest of her friends were nice to me, but Alison was the one I really hung out with the most, and she was a separate friend from Brittany and Amanda—not for any real reason except that that's just how high school works sometimes. You have friends from different groups, and trying to combine them can get weird. It wasn't a big deal.

Anyway, we were at her house one day when we grabbed a handful of Oreos from her kitchen and went up to her bedroom. I immediately noticed a new poster on her wall.

It was a portrait of two girls, the most beautiful women I'd ever seen. They looked eerily alike, and both of them were made up pretty emo, with tons of black eyeliner, dark red lipstick, and blue and black nail polish. One of them had long black hair, and the other's was shorter with blond streaks. They had fishnet stockings on their arms, tons of jewelry, and looked all-around badass.

"Those are the Veronicas," Alison said. "They're twin sisters and have a band together. Here, check them out."

She went over to her computer and clicked on their My-Space page. We watched a video for their song "4ever." And then I made her play it again. And again. And again. I was obsessed. The song was fun and catchy ("Come on baby, we ain't gonna live forever / Let me show you all the things that we could do!"). I couldn't get it out of my head. As soon as I got home, I looked them up online and printed out every photo I could find of them. I taped the images to my walls while listening to their songs on repeat until I'd memorized every lyric.

I learned all I could about their personalities. Jess is the older twin, by one minute, and she's a little edgier and darker than Lisa, who in my mind came across as sweet and kind in interviews. I decided that she was my favorite and the one I should have a crush on.

I became a hard-core fan. Every day after school, I'd spam the hell out of their MySpace page, writing about how much I loved them. I hoped that if my comments showed up the most, then they'd notice me. Basically, their entire MySpace page was just me geeking out, raving about them and begging them to post on my own page, but I never got any sort of response. (I find this extremely funny now, because some of you reading this have done the exact same thing to me on Twitter. You know who you are!) So when I found out they were playing a concert in Worcester, only about half an hour away, I just about died. I was determined to meet Lisa.

Alison's mom drove me, her, a girl named Rachel (a childhood friend who I'm pretty sure knew about my home life situation without my ever telling her—she was just intuitive like that), Alison's older sister, and two other friends to the show. I insisted that we get there early so that we could be right in front of the stage, but there was already a line by the time we got there. I ran as fast as I could when the doors opened but there was still a crowd about three people deep ahead of me and no more room for me to elbow people out of the way.

There were two opening acts that night. I don't remember who the first band was, but the second was a bunch of kids nobody had ever heard of called the Jonas Brothers. (Ha!) I stood there with my arms folded, glaring at those geeks because all I wanted was for the Veronicas to get out onstage. I eventually loosened up a little bit and grudgingly had to admit that the Jonas Brothers sounded pretty good.

After they finally left the stage, a guy walked out to introduce the Veronicas. It took me a second to recognize him, but realized it was Ricky Ullman, the star of one of my favorite Disney Channel shows, *Phil of the Future*. I started screaming uncontrollably, and I might have been hyperventilating a little too, because the whole world seemed to slow down and advance forward frame by frame, like I was watching a movie by hitting the Pause and Play button over and over again.

Lisa and Jess strode out onstage, grabbed the mikes, and launched into a song. I was jumping at least a foot off the ground in time with the music, pumping my fists in the air and shouting the lyrics along with them. And even though I wasn't in the very front row, I focused my eyes on Lisa, willing her to see me, and she did! I didn't care if I seemed like a crazy stalker; I was in a euphoric state of pubescent delirium. I had borrowed my mom's good camera and stopped dancing and singing only long enough to snap a few photos before starting to shriek again.

Midway through the concert, all of my insanity paid off. They ended a song and Lisa locked eyes with me, pointed, and spoke into the microphone: "We'd like to dedicate this next one to . . . YOU!!" She and Jess launched into their song "Speechless," which is exactly what I was. I could hear all of my friends screaming my name and freaking out around me, but I was frozen. I saw Lisa and Jess reach their arms out to me, and the crowd parted. They pulled me onstage and continued to sing. "Feels like I have always known you. And I swear I've dreamt about you." I stood there like an idiot, swinging my head back and forth to look at each one of them. They were even more beautiful up close. I looked out into the audience and saw my friends below practically clawing at their faces with excitement. I'd stepped into an actual waking dream. I felt hands on my arms and realized they were leading me back down off the stage so I hopped off and turned around, finally standing at the very front.

They finished the song and Lisa leaned down and pointed at the side of her face, mouthing something that I couldn't hear but what looked like *Give me a kiss*. And so I kissed her cheek. "No," she said into the microphone so everyone in the auditorium could hear. "I asked *what's your name?*"

Everyone roared with laughter.

"Joey," I whimpered.

"Ooooh. Joey's cute," Lisa said and then she winked at me before standing back up and starting a new song. The thrill of what had just happened quickly overrode any embarrassment over the kiss, and for the rest of the show I felt like I was still up there onstage with them, dancing my butt off.

There was a meet-and-greet upstairs at the venue after the show, but since we were so close to the front of the stage, it meant we were near the end of the line by the time we got up there. We stood there forever, too excited to be impatient, and at one point Joe Jonas walked by and spotted me. He rushed over and exclaimed, "How cool was that, to be pulled up onstage!"

Obviously I had no idea that he would one day be as famous as he is, and so I couldn't have cared less about talking to him. "It was pretty cool," I answered, and then turned back to Alison to continue gushing about the experience. (Hey, Joe. Feel free to talk to me now. I promise I'll be nicer!)

When it was finally our turn at the Veronicas' table, they broke into huge smiles when they saw me. "Oh my god, it's you!" Jess said.

"We love you," Lisa added.

"I love you too. Will you sign my poster?"

"Of course, sweetie," Jess said, and they scribbled all over it—not just their signatures but things like "marry me!" and "you're awesome!" They both hugged me and I took some selfies with them, and it was basically the best night of my life up to that point.

It's crazy: *they* follow *me* on Twitter now, and we keep in touch from time to time. It was my first experience with a celebrity. I know a lot of people say that you should never meet your idols, that you'll be disappointed. But the Veronicas showed me how to treat a fan. If someone has invested the time to pay attention to your work and appreciate what you do, I think you owe it to him or her to show appreciation back. I will always treasure my experience at the Veronicas concert, but I value what they taught me that night even more. I had no clue just how important that lesson would be in my future.

Ten Bands That Will Always Be in My iTunes Library

The Veronicas

Marina and the Diamonds

Lana Del Rey

Panic! At the Disco

Ellie Goulding

Walk the Moon

Mika

Aly and AJ

Katy Perry

Paramore

Chapter 5

My First Girlfriend (and Other Disasters)

Now that I finally had a solid group of friends in place, it was a lot easier to deal with bullying. There were still occasional jerks in the classroom or on the bus who made fun of my feminine qualities, but by tenth grade, it wasn't happening every day. That was the year I started noticing a girl named Ali in my history class. She was short and cute, with dark brown hair and a closet full of Hollister clothes. We didn't talk or anything, but I soon found out from another friend of hers named Nicki that she thought I was cute and liked me.

I immediately got all flustered and blushed a deep red. A girl actually *liked* me?? That had never happened before. Most girls saw me as just a friend. The next day I gathered up the courage to introduce myself. We exchanged AIM screen names and started chatting every day after school. I began to get excited about the thought of having a girlfriend. We got along great—we both loved Hollister and being preppy! (I'm cringing right now—I mean, what more do you need in a relationship, right?) Nicki told me that Ali was getting impatient and wondered when I was going to ask her out. I had no idea! I was scared! In our high school, asking someone out didn't mean a date. It meant that you were boyfriend and girlfriend.

The tension finally got to be too much. We were walking in

the hall together, and I could feel my throat starting to close up. I knew it was go time: "So, Ali, since I really like you, and you really like me, would you be my girlfriend?"

She squealed and stopped in the middle of the sea of students swarming around us and hugged me so hard. "Yes," she said. "Of course!" Then we went our separate ways to each of our classes. That afternoon we both went home and each changed our AIM profile names to "Joey ♥ Ali" and "Ali ♥ Joey." (So lame. So high school.) Other than that, nothing else was really that different between us.

After a couple of days, we were walking to get bagels together at lunch when she suddenly asked if we could make out sometime. Gulp. I had never been kissed, let alone made out with someone, and I had NO IDEA how it was done. But I put on my bravest face and said, "Yeah, that would be fun." I was shaking with terror inside.

I managed to delay the make-out session for a few days, and that hesitation cost me. I was at Brittany's house one afternoon and noticed that Ali was signed on to AIM. I wrote "Hi," and she immediately wrote back, "We need to talk."

I felt my heart drop into my toes and told Brittany to turn around and not look at the computer while Ali and I chatted. She dumped me, saying that she wasn't ready for a relationship but that maybe sometime in the future she would be. I innocently held on to those words as if she actually meant them. I told myself that I would wait for her, but I was still so sad and embarrassed that I couldn't even tell Brittany what had just happened.

But when we got to school the next day, the news had already spread. Everyone knew. Alison ended up grabbing me in the hallway and pulling me to one side. "There's something you need to know," she whispered. "Ali broke up with you because a bunch of guys told her that you are gay and she was just being your beard."

Beard? What the hell was she talking about? What did my facial hair, or lack thereof, have to do with any of this? That thought quickly disappeared as what she said actually sank in: Ali had dumped me because she thought I was gay. I was so embarrassed, but that embarrassment quickly turned to anger. All I could think was: *How dare people spread rumors about me!*

Later that day in history class, Ali wouldn't even make eye contact with me. A guy I barely recognized was sitting behind me, and he started whispering horrible things in my ear, calling me a faggot and asking me if I liked it up the butt. I finally had enough. I slammed my chair back, stood up, and turned around to face him.

"WHO ARE YOU?" I yelled. "I don't even know your name. You are NO ONE to me."

I sat back down, shaking. *Whoa, what just came over me?* The whole class stared in stunned silence. I don't think anyone expected that sort of outburst from me. That lame jerk kept his mouth shut for the rest of the year whenever he was around me.

My self-confidence was growing, but there was still one big thing I was grappling with: my return to SPED classes. The school had decided that my learning disability was still holding me back. In high school, the SPED classes were called something different—an Individualized Education Program. But the IEP still carried the same stigma as SPED. I had most of my classes with other students, but for one period a day, I would go and study with a different set of students who, like me, had trouble with some of the basics. Just like when I was younger, I had managed to keep it a secret, until one day I was outed. Only this time, it was a teacher who spilled the beans instead of another student.

It happened in Spanish class, and if it had been any other teacher, the situation could have been easily avoided. But this teacher was notoriously mean. I made an honest mistake, handing in an assignment one day early instead of the one that was actually due that particular day. I had done the homework, just gotten the dates mixed up. I asked if I could switch the days around, promising to turn in that day's assignment the following day. It wasn't like I hadn't done any work. I kept trying to explain my mix-up, but she wouldn't even look at me when she told me she wouldn't accept the work and that she was going to give me an incomplete for what was due that day. I started to plead my case again when she finally looked up and said loudly, "Joey, just go to your IEP. I don't have time for this."

I was frozen, then flooded with embarrassment. But just like when the kid kept calling me a fag, my shame quickly turned to anger. I shoved my chair hard against the desk as I stood up and marched to the door. Just before I left, I spun around and said, "You know what? No. I'm not going. I'm going to the principal's office to let him know how much of a bitch you are."

I couldn't believe I'd actually just called a teacher a bitch, but screw it—that's how I felt. Who was she to reveal that private part of my life to everyone? All the teachers knew I was in an IEP, but they were supposed to keep it confidential.

As I stormed off to the principal's office in a fit of rage and with tears welling up in my eyes, I passed the photocopy room, where Amanda's mother worked. She saw the frustration on my face as I walked by and rushed out into the hallway.

"Honey, what's wrong?"

I explained what had just happened, and she became furious.

"She did what?" she asked in disbelief. "That's not right. You need to go talk to the guidance counselor."

And so I did, and then my parents got involved, and in the end a bunch of other kids came forward with reports of inappropriate behavior from this teacher and she ended up resigning. I was happy I didn't have to deal with her anymore, but it didn't change the fact that most of the school now knew I was considered less intelligent than everyone else. I became determined to prove that I was just as smart as them, and so I began to study extra hard.

For the first time, I started to get into science, and I began reading in my spare time, devouring the *His Dark Materials* trilogy. The extra work paid off, and I finally got out of IEP. I felt free. I no longer had to let this label that I'd had for most of my life define me. I worked hard so I could prove that I can make something of myself and not be a victim of circumstance. And not only did I get out of IEP, I got placed in the Honors English class. It wasn't easy, but the most rewarding things in life never are. More and more, I was seeing results from my actions and efforts. It was like discovering some sort of secret superpower. All I had to do was put my mind to something, and I could make it happen!

In response to this new confidence, Bob gave me a digital camcorder for my fifteenth birthday, so I could actually import the videos Brit and I were making onto my computer to edit. Bob had always supported my creative endeavors and loved my little videos, and it had partly been his belief in me that helped me find the drive to get out of the IEP.

The camcorder arrived in my life right around the time that YouTube debuted, and Brittany and I were immediately hooked. The site was filled with silly, dumb videos just like the ones we made for fun; only these ones were up on the Internet for everyone else to see and engage with. We knew it was perfect for us, but we had no clue how huge of an impact the site would end up having on our lives.

Five Essential Study Tips

When I started working my butt off to try and get out of SPED classes, these were my top five study tricks. And they're not just for people who have learning disabilities; everyone can benefit from them.

1. Make flash cards. I loved making flash cards for learning things like vocabulary definitions and equations. Not only do you get to pretend you're on a game show, but the actual act of making the cards can help cement the information in your brain.

2. Use mnemonic devices. These are genius, and I used them A LOT. Basically, you just take a chunk of information that you need to memorize and turn it into something that your particular brain will better remember. A classic one is the order of the planets from the sun—just create any sentence using the first letter of each planet in the order of words. So, assuming Pluto is still off the list by the time this book comes out, you can use something like "My Very Easy Method, Just Sleep Until Noon." (Mercury, Venus, Earth, Mars, Jupiter, Saturn, Uranus, Neptune.)

3. Use a reward system. If you plan to devote an extra hour every day to studying, be sure to devote another hour to doing something special for yourself. Like if your parents limit the amount of time you're allowed to play video games, see if you can get them to let you play an extra hour for each additional hour you spend hitting the books.

4. Find a quiet space. Resist distracting temptations at all costs. I always had to study in a totally different room from my computer because it was too easy to think, "Oh, I'll just look this one thing up," and then three hours later find myself emerging from a YouTube hole. Stick to quiet places like the library or the dining room table.

5. Choose a study buddy. It helps to have someone with the same educational goals keep you on track. But keep in mind that your BFF might not be the best person. Make sure it's someone who won't distract you. And it's great if it's someone who happens to be comfortable with a subject that you find difficult.

Chapter 6
YouTube Calling

Brittany and I quickly became obsessed with a YouTube channel run by a girl named Brookers. She lived in Massachusetts like us, which made the idea of being on YouTube all the more real and accessible. More important, she had the same whack-job sense of humor that we did, so we knew that there was an audience for our style. She had around forty or fifty thousand subscribers, which was huge in 2007. One of her videos was a recap of the first Harry Potter movie that devolves into a weird heavy metal song. In another, she prank-calls a restaurant and manages to keep her victim on the line for nearly eight minutes. Genius. I had found my new creative outlet.

Brittany and I decided to start our own channel to post videos to, and we needed a name. We were sitting at my kitchen table, and I was doing random Google image searches for inspiration when my cat, Pookie, jumped up on my lap.

"I know," Brittany said. "Pookie Productions!"

"That's a terrible idea."

Somehow I'd landed on a page full of GIFs and one caught my eye—a tree that bloomed full of green leaves on one side and was barren with snowflakes falling on it on the other, representing two seasons. Something about it clicked in my brain. I'd been spending a lot of time playing the game *World of Warcraft*, because like *RuneScape* before it, I loved that I could

70

wander through an entirely made-up universe. One of my favorite places to go was an area called WinterSpring. (If you want further proof that I'm a total nerd, it's located in northeastern Kalimdor and is home to the goblin city Everlook. There are a lot of demons in the southern region, so watch out.)

"What about WinterSpring Productions?" I asked, showing Brittany the picture and explaining the origin. "This picture could make a really good logo that goes perfectly with the name."

She shrugged. "Sure." Brittany always indulged my weird ideas.

And so our channel was born. We quickly shortened the name to WinterSpringPro (or WSP), because those last two syllables just seemed to get in the way.

The only problem was that we didn't know what our first official video should be. I wanted it to be cool and really stand out. It needed to make some sort of splash since it was our debut. Brittany and I spent hours on the computer watching the other kinds of videos that people were posting; one that had gone viral was basically just a piece of fruit moving across a countertop via stop-motion animation.

"We could do that with our bodies," I said. "Like, make us move without it seeming like we were actually moving. It would look so much cooler than this."

Brittany was into the idea, and so on the last day of our sophomore year, we spent nine hours recording our first official YouTube video, "Humanation." The premise was simple: wake up, get dressed, get breakfast, go outside, jump around, all in stop motion and set to a technobeat.

Unfortunately, we happened to pick one of the hottest days of the year to record it, so we spent more time indoors than out, and when we were outside, we tried to film in the shade whenever possible. Once we were finished, I spent another five hours editing it, uploaded it to YouTube, and waited for the comments and views to start blowing up.

Insert sound of crickets.

NOBODY was watching our video. So I decided to be pro-active. I made up a bunch of fake YouTube accounts and started leaving positive feedback for us under different names. Stuff like "OMG COOL VID!!!" and "How did they do that???" and "Best video EVER!!" (Don't judge me, guys. It's not easy to establish yourself!)

Next, I began spamming other YouTubers' comments sections, writing stuff like, "If you think this video is cool, you HAVE to check out WinterSpringPro!" I wasn't afraid to work it, which was weird for me, because in real life I could still be shy and socially awkward, even with all of my new friends and growing confidence. But it was easy to be aggressive online. It wasn't face-to-face; I could hide behind a screen.

And it worked. Suddenly people started watching and giving "Humanation" five stars, leaving really nice comments and, best of all, subscribing. Subscriptions meant that they really believed in us and wanted to see more. Seeing that someone from across the world was watching a video that we'd made in Marlborough, Massachusetts, was surreal and my first glimpse of how powerful the Internet is at connecting people.

We made sure to return the favor: if anyone asked us to watch one of his or her videos, we would, and we'd leave positive feedback. It was a give-and-take system of goodwill, and even though there were a lot of crap videos, I felt that if someone took the time to say something nice about us online, it was only fair to do the same thing in return.

Once the views and subscriptions started pouring in, we

realized we needed to step up our game. We posted around twelve videos in all over the summer break. Some of them were really simple—footage of us jumping into a swimming pool, but in reverse so it looked like we were flying out of the water. Other times we got really high-concept, like *The Joey Show*, where I played a deranged talk show host who used a mop as a microphone while documenting Brittany's made-up tragic life.

By the end of the summer, our videos were averaging around ten thousand views, and we had almost two thousand subscribers. How crazy is that?! I don't think it would be that easy for a newbie anymore; it was sort of the Wild West of You-Tube at that time, and the market wasn't as crowded. We were lucky that we got in early, but a lot of it also had to do with developing friendly and supportive relationships with You-Tubers who were just like us—basically, a bunch of nobodies who shared our bizarro sensibilities.

On the first day of eleventh grade, my English teacher asked everyone in the class to give a presentation on what we did over the summer, and when I explained what Brittany and I had done, everyone was really impressed. The same people who used to bully me when I was younger watched the videos and told me they loved them. They were probably still making fun of me behind my back, but I didn't care, because I was also getting recognition from people I knew genuinely liked what we were doing: the underclassmen.

I could tell from the WSP comments section that a lot of our viewers were younger, and it turned out that some of them went to our school. My English class that year was located in the wing that housed the eighth graders, and one week I started noticing a trio of girls who always grinned and pointed at me whenever I passed them in the hallway. They made me nervous: I couldn't tell if they had a crush on me or were making fun of me for some reason.

One day they finally surrounded me outside class.

"We love your videos," one of them said with a giggle.

"You're so funny," another one said, nervously twirling a heart-shaped pendant around one finger.

"Can I have your autograph?" the third one asked, handing me her red backpack and a black pen.

I still wasn't sure if they were just teasing me or if they were legitimately fans of WinterSpringPro. It seemed too bizarre that strangers in my school were watching my videos and liking them enough to ask for my autograph.

"Sure," I said. "Thanks so much for watching." As I scribbled my name on the girl's satchel, I kept waiting for them to burst out laughing, like maybe it was all just a big joke. But they were totally serious, and from then on, they always waved and said hi to me whenever I passed them in the hallway and complimented me whenever a new video went up. It was my first experience with real-life audience interaction, and it made me feel that Brittany and I were doing something right. Maybe there was a bigger reason for us to be creating our odd little videos than just a sense of wanting to be seen. Our videos were actually making these girls, and clearly other people too, happy.

I signed up for a television production class that our school offered, and the quality of our videos got much better. It was the first time it dawned on me that I could make a living out of my love for videos and become an editor or director.

By the end of the school year, we had posted twenty videos, and for our one-year anniversary, we celebrated by filming "Humanation 2," a much more elaborate version of our first stop-motion video: we used our bodies as if they were cars zipping around the school and playground.

Around this same time, YouTube announced the Partner Program. If you were accepted, you'd get an ad banner on your channel and share the profits based on the number of views and subscribers. We were having fun doing WSP as a hobby, but we worked hard at it, so the idea of making money off it seemed too good to be true. Our application was rejected: we didn't have enough subscribers. But the people at YouTube were encouraging and told us we were getting close and that we should try reapplying in two months. So we spent the summer working our butts off, hustling for subscribers, and putting even more effort into our production values.

YouTube was getting bigger and more popular, and we started to pay close attention to trends. We noticed that a lot of the videos that tended to go viral referenced pop culture in some way, so we started incorporating outside influences into our work, but with our own spin. For example, we took a clip of Lisa Nova, one of our favorite big-time YouTubers, and inserted her into a sketch about the Jonas Brothers going to public high school. I borrowed a bunch of life-size cardboard cut-outs of the band from Alison, who ended up becoming a huge fan of theirs after we went to the Veronicas' concert, and animated Brittany's and my lips into their mouths to make them speak. We also shot a fake trailer for *Saw 6* (although we accidentally used the roman numeral for five in the title credit), where we were chained together in a basement and forced to play fill-in-the-letter word games. Another mistake from that one: we flashed cards throughout the clip that were full of spelling errors like, "Sacrafices Will Be Made" and "Unspeakable Torcher Will Occur!" (Thanks again, paint chips!)

We racked up a lot more subscribers, and by the end of the summer; it paid off: YouTube informed us that we'd made partnership. We of course assumed we'd become millionaires immediately and were pretty bummed when our first check came in for one hundred dollars, which we split. Still, it was an incredible feeling to get paid to do what we loved.

As our channel slowly grew larger, we started communicating with other YouTubers. One of the first was a hyperactive, temper-tantrum-prone kid named Fred Figglehorn, with an eerily high-pitched voice who was the alter ego of a guy named Lucas Cruikshank. He was extremely popular online, and Brittany and I watched his videos regularly. We managed to get his cell phone number through a friend of a friend and started prank-calling him. At first we'd just giggle nervously and hang up, but soon we started talking to him as if we were old friends.

"Hey, man! How's it going?"

"Oh, good," he'd stammer, sounding a little confused.

"I'm so hungry. Are you? We should go grab something to eat."

"Wait, sorry, who is this?"

I'd laugh. "Oh come on. You know who it is. So what do you think? Olive Garden, say, around eight o'clock?"

"I've already got dinner plans," he said as we tried not to crack up.

"Oh, well, next time!"

Brittany and I alternated doing a few different versions of that exchange for about a week. It was actually really sweet that he pretended as long as he did, not wanting to hurt the feelings of his "friends" by not recognizing their voices. He finally got fed up, though, and demanded to know who we were.

Brittany was the one on the phone when he finally snapped, but he laughed when she told him it had been WinterSpring-Pro calling him the entire time. We couldn't believe he actually knew who we were, and he was a really great sport about the whole thing. We'd just filmed a spoof of an appearance he'd done on *Hannah Montana* and asked if he'd be willing to tweet about it or mention it in one of his videos. But our version made fun of the show a little *too* much, and he didn't think his manager would appreciate it. Still, now that he was talking to us, we were desperate to get him to mention our channel somehow since he had such a huge audience. We came up with an idea to contact as many other YouTubers as we could to do a little short film congratulating him on reaching 1 million subscribers—he had been one of the first YouTubers to do so.

Sure, I'd tweet about that, he texted when we pitched the idea. *That would be awesome!*

We reached out first to Shane Dawson, a YouTuber we both really loved, and he was immediately game to shoot something for us. Then we reached out to another favorite, iJustine, and as soon as we got her on board, the rest just fell into place. We e-mailed more of our favorite YouTubers, and they were all really into the idea. I'd like to say it was done purely in the spirit of supporting other talent, but although we all genuinely liked each other, there was an unspoken understanding that by collaborating, we'd be spreading our own brand across new platforms; we hoped everyone would gain more subscribers.

The concept of the video was that as soon as Fred reached 1 million subscribers he had become an all-powerful, vengeful being who started killing off other YouTubers one by one by shooting death rays out of his disembodied head. Fred tweeted about it and the video blew up with over half a million views.

During this whole time, even though we had a huge audience of our own, I had continued to audition for school plays with varying degrees of success. In tenth grade I managed to get into the chorus of the spring musical of *Guys and Dolls*. I played a drunk guy who stumbles onto stage and utters one line: "What vulgar jewelry!" It was awkward but better than nothing. My junior year, I got a role in a student-written play, "Teenage Dream." It predated the Katy Perry song and was all about the nightmares of being a teenager. I played a little kid who, along with his brother, spends an evening terrorizing their babysitter (What is it with school plays about psycho little kids??). At that point I was deep into WinterSpringPro, so my confidence was way higher than it had ever been before—so much so that I convinced my "brother" to go off-script with me on opening night.

We added in a bunch of our own lines and improvised a physical fight. But the whole thing backfired, and instead of enhancing the show, it just caused us to lose our place once our new bits were over. I found myself standing on the stage in silence, sweating under the lights, desperately trying to remember what my real lines were while people out in the audience coughed nervously. Thank goodness the girl who played the babysitter managed to steer us back on track. The whole ridiculous episode made me appreciate how much control I had over acting in, directing, and editing my own videos on YouTube.

Our First Fan Letter

After we started getting some decent views, we opened a post office box for fan mail. We waited about a week, and then headed back to see what had come in. We thought it would be stuffed, but it was completely empty. We waited another week, and by that time there were a few letters. We freaked out and wrote handwritten letters back to everyone. We even included an autographed photo of us. Friendship bracelets were a pretty big thing at the time, and we got a ton sent to us. I still have them all!

What Makes a Creative Partnership Work

When you're working with another person on a creative project, it's important to make sure that you each have equal responsibilities, so neither of you feels that you are doing more work than the other. While brainstorming, clear your mind of everything else and bounce ideas off each other until something sparks. Build on each other's ideas. And if your partner tosses out an idea that you don't think works, make sure to say why you don't think it works rather than just shooting it down. This will help get you both to develop a shared vision.

How to Make a Viral Video

There are no instructions. I'd be a billionaire if I knew how to do this because the elements that cause a video to go viral are varied and random, though usually it has to do with an undercurrent of what's happening culturally at large. You can basically chalk it up to posting the right video at the right time, and there's nothing more painful than watching a branded video that you can tell was made in an obvious attempt to go viral. The cringe factor is equal to having your weird uncle show up at a school dance as a chaperone and start moonwalking. Now <u>that</u> is a video that would probably go viral.

Five Things to Remember While Doing a School Play

1. Never ad-lib.
2. Don't talk over other people's lines.
3. Always listen to your director.
4. Make friends with the stage crew so they don't mess with you.
5. If you start to freak out on opening night, remember this: the lights are going to be so bright that you can barely see the audience anyway.

My Favorite Musicals

The Book of Mormon. There was a Mormon family in one of my neighborhoods growing up, and they always seemed mysterious to me. This play answered a lot of my questions about their religion, but even better, it made me laugh my ass off.

Singing in the Rain. I saw a high school production of this a few towns over when I was young, and the songs have stuck with me. I also loved learning about the old Hollywood transition from silent film to talkies.

Anything Goes. This was another high school production that I wasn't cast in, and I will always consider it the one that got away. I'm still determined to sing "You're the Top" in front of an audience someday.

The Wizard of Oz. I watched this movie countless times when I was little, and I think it must have been the origin of my obsession with fantasy stories.

The Lion King. The way the stage production transformed an animated movie into those awesome, huge puppets is pure magic. Hakuna matata, baby.

Chapter 7

Little Squish

YouTube wasn't the only bundle of joy that came into my life during high school. By the time I turned fifteen, my mother had sobered up and reunited with Bob. I'm not sure what the catalyst was, but I didn't care. I was just happy to have her back, plus we moved into a nicer apartment. Our home life had finally smoothed out into a stable environment, and she and Bob began trying to have a child of their own again. They had been trying throughout their marriage, but my mom suffered a series of miscarriages. It was a heartbreaking period for all of us, but she never once slid back into drinking.

She and Bob kept trying, and by the time she told me that she was pregnant again, I knew that her chances of carrying the baby through to term were good (by that point she had stopped telling people each time she got pregnant since the miscarriages were so frequent). But this time was different—she was really far along and the baby was looking healthy.

It seemed crazy that at fifteen years old, I was going to have another sibling. I couldn't wait to have someone to boss around the way Nicole had done to me, only I knew I would never take it as far as she did. I'd tease him for sure, but I also planned to be kind and gentle and act like a proper mentor from the get-go. I was ready. Mom being pregnant also meant that I didn't have to worry about her starting to drink again. I knew she wouldn't do anything to endanger the baby. It brought an even greater

83

sense of peace into my life. My baby brother became a symbol of our happy new life on the horizon.

Once Jett arrived, the whole family fell immediately in love with him. He was tiny and squishy and adorable, like a bald little alien wrapped in blankets. Everyone doted on him, but as we got closer to his first birthday, we began to notice that he wasn't developing as fast as other kids his age in terms of his communication skills. Our apartment was on the second floor of a house, and the little girl who lived downstairs, who was a bit older than him, was already babbling away with our family whenever we'd pass her in the stairwell or see her in the yard, whereas Jett would just stare at us with his big blue eyes, looking lost whenever we talked to him.

My mom and Bob took him to see various doctors, all of whom said that he would grow out of it and talk when he was ready, but after another year of silence, it was apparent that there was definitely something wrong. We tried everything to get him to interact with us, but he was withdrawn and shy. He would mumble at us but wouldn't form any actual words. Mom enrolled him in weekly classes with a specialist who tried to get him to open up, but nothing worked.

He was finally diagnosed as autistic, which was sort of a relief because armed with that knowledge, we could at least start learning about ways to bring him more into our lives, and vice versa. But it also got me really worried. It was pretty clear that he was going to have to go to special education classes, and after what I had gone through, I didn't want him to have to experience any of the same feelings of not belonging. Luckily, by the time he was old enough to go to school, my parents had found a place that wasn't mixed in with the general population—an institution specifically for children with autism.

Jett wants to respond to people, but he can't. He can understand what we say to him, but is able to answer only with small grunts and pointing. We developed a sort of shorthand communication style, like if I was playing with him and stopped, he'd take my hand and guide it back to whatever we were playing with to tell me that he wanted to keep at it.

My parents discovered a whole bunch of apps that were created specifically for kids with autism, so they bought Jett an iPad. It opened up a whole new world for all of us. He could point at pictures of things in order to tell us what he wanted. Now, if he is hungry for an apple, all he has to do is point at a picture of one. But there was one time when he stuck his iPad in the microwave and turned it on. (I didn't know you couldn't put metal in a microwave until I was sixteen.)

I became Jett's babysitter. He had such special needs that we didn't trust many other people to watch him. It was a big responsibility, and it could get frustrating. I wanted to be a normal teenager and go out and have fun all the time, not have to watch him every day. But his cute little face made it all worth it, plus I secretly loved having an excuse to watch all the kids' shows he did!

All of my original wishes about having a little brother to tease went out the window. I only wanted to protect him. (Okay, I'd still tease him a little bit. He hated having his hair cut, so sometimes I'd chase him around the house making scissor motions with my fingers. But he always knew it was just a game.) He loved being tickled, and I made up nicknames for him like Jetty and Little Squish.

It's tough to know that I'll never be able to have a real conversation with him. I want to be able to teach him things about life that I have learned and pass along all of my big brother wisdom. I can still do that to a degree, but his life is going to be very different from mine and Nicole's, and the fact is that I know he will probably end up being the one to teach *me* lessons about getting past adversity. In fact, he already has. Every time I find myself getting shy around someone now, I force myself to get over it because I know I'm lucky enough to be able to actually say what's on my mind. Having a little brother with autism has taught me much about patience, resilience, and unconditional love. And he is going to continue to teach me about communication for the rest of my life, since I know that we will constantly develop new ways to interact with each other as we both get older. I can't wait to see the man he will grow up to be.

What Is Autism?

Autism is a general term to describe varying degrees of brain development disorders. They are usually characterized by difficulty in communicating, awkward social interactions, and repetitive behavior. One in sixty-eight American children fall somewhere on the autism spectrum—a number that's increased greatly in the past forty years. You can learn much more about it at autismspeaks.org or autismsciencefoundation.org.

A Couple of Great iPad Apps for Autistic Kids

If you have a sibling with autism, Proloquo2go is an app with over 14,000 symbols that help autistic kids build language skills. It costs almost $200, which sounds crazy for an app, but you can't really put a price on being able to effectively communicate with a family member. Another cool resource (and a free one) is Autism Apps. Download it to search over thirty learning categories and curate a bunch of apps that will be appropriate for the specific needs of your loved one.

Chapter 8

So Alone

By the time my college application phase arrived, I knew that I wanted to go to film school, and I thought that all of my YouTube experience gave me a competitive edge. In the guidance counselor's office one day, as I was flipping through brochures about the country's top film programs, I discovered the school of my dreams, Emerson College. It's in Boston so it was close to home, and the stats were incredible—many Emerson alumni have gone on to work on films like *Watchmen* and television shows like *Friends* and *The Colbert Report*. One grad had even won a Pulitzer. I scheduled a campus tour, and once I visited, I fell in love with it. The buildings were sleek and modern, and I could feel its creative energy in my bones. I knew that I had to get in, that it was the place that would allow me to follow my dreams. I genuinely believed that the only way I would succeed in life was if I got into this school.

The problem was that Emerson is a hard school to get into, and although my grades were much better now that I was out of the IEP, I knew I needed something that would stand out on my application. The film department requires applicants to submit a video, so I decided to shoot a seriously kick-ass short horror film.

I hated scary movies as a child, but I eventually grew to love them. People who are into this genre have all sorts of different reasons for liking it (gore hounds are the worst), but for me, I got into them because I was such a scaredy-cat on my own. I already saw dark and spooky things everywhere I looked, so I was hooked whenever a creepy movie came on TV. I devoured them, even when they gave me nightmares for weeks. As I got older, I began to appreciate that power. Anything that could leave such a lasting impression meant that it was striking some sort of primal nerve, and I wanted to be able to tap into that with my own work.

I thought the movie was the best piece I'd ever done when I made it, but watching it now makes me want to pluck my eyeballs out. Brittany and I shot it in the middle of winter, on a day of freezing rain. The basic premise was this: A girl disappears a few days before two high school students venture out into the woods to shoot photographs of trees for extra credit (hence the movie's name, "Extra Credit"). A murderer in a faceless white mask is on the loose, hunting us down in the woods. Brittany gets butchered, but I escape to the car, only to find that the killer is waiting for me in the backseat. Fade to black.

The acting was pretty horrendous, and one of our camera tripods even shows up in the background at one point. But all I saw was my ticket to the school of my dreams.

I didn't get in. And I was devastated. Actually *devastated* isn't a strong enough word. The rejection felt like a crushing attack on my abilities, and for a while I thought my creative life was over. I figured that if Emerson didn't like me, I wasn't worth anything. I'd put so much stock in that school being the driving force that would dictate my future, and after the admissions department basically let me know that I wasn't good enough for the college, I didn't think I was good enough for anyone. Obviously that didn't end up being the case, but I often think about that period of my life whenever I get down about something not working out the way I'd planned. The fact is, I got over it. I picked myself up, brushed off my shoulders, and kept moving forward. It wasn't the end of the world, even if it felt like it at the time. No matter how much a situation can suck, it's ultimately your choice as to whether you're going to let it drag you down.

I had applied to four other schools as backups and ended up getting into Fitchburg, a state school about forty minutes away that has a film and video concentration. My friend Amanda ended up getting in too, so I'd have someone there I already knew, and we were excited to start this new part of our lives together. We knew that college was going to be the best thing ever (even if it wasn't Emerson). And though we couldn't be roommates, we promised to hang out as much as possible.

Brittany decided to go to a nearby community college, and we pledged to keep working on WSP even though we'd be apart. Despite getting rejected by my top-choice school, I was starting to really believe in myself again based on all the positive feedback we continued to get on our videos. And besides, I knew I could always reapply to Emerson the following year and transfer.

•   •   •

College started out great, with the best part being my newly found freedom. I was finally on my own and able to make my own schedule. And not only was Amanda with me, I'd already made a new friend before the first day of classes from a Facebook page that was set up for incoming freshmen. I started chatting with a pretty girl named Chloe who mentioned that she was also going to do the film and video concentration.

Fitchburg isn't located in the greatest neighborhood, but

the campus has lots of green lawns and old brick buildings that look like mansions. My dorm room was a forced triple— basically a double that the school added bunk beds to in order to squeeze one extra person in. I arrived first and got to call dibs on the bunk bed that had an empty space beneath it. I moved my desk under it and created a little home office for myself. I plastered the walls with *Futurama* posters and made up the bed with a new bright green comforter and matching pillows.

My roommates were classic male college stereotypes—the football player and the stoner. Their idea of decorating was slapping a Bob Marley poster and a giant ad for Jack Daniels on the wall. Since I was finally away from a place where I'd been teased my entire life for being feminine, I decided that this was time for a New Joey. So for the first two days, every time I spoke, I dropped my voice down two octaves and made sure not to wave my arms around when I talked like I usually did.

The football player got transferred to a different dorm after the first week, and since I got along better with the stoner, I felt that I could drop the dude act and just be my normal self. Although I was totally not into weed, we got along pretty well. He was really mellow (OBVIOUSLY) and basically let me be. But our suite had three other rooms in it, so I was still stuck with six other guys, all of them jocks, whom I had to share a bathroom with. The guys were disgusting. The bathroom had a permanent stench of beer, mold, and barf, and after just one week, the sink was plastered in mysterious thick goo. (To this day I refuse to live in a place where I have to share a bathroom with another person.)

The other big problem was that after I introduced the stoner to Amanda, they almost immediately began dating. Every night I'd have to fall asleep to the sound of their lips smacking in the dark.

91

Amanda also really got along with Chloe, the girl I had met on Facebook. The three of us became a team, almost like what Amanda and I had with Brittany in high school. In the beginning, we spent a lot of time together and formed a little family, since we all felt lonely being away from our actual ones. Every night we'd get dinner together, and then we'd either play video games or go off-campus to check out parties. But I grew tired of going out really fast. Being stuck in a packed room full of smashed strangers in a trashy apartment was not my idea of a good time. Every time I saw someone stumble, all I could think about was my mother. One night after a party, Chloe came back to our dorm and started throwing up in the bathroom. Instead of trying to take care of her, I just stayed in my bed and didn't even offer to help hold her hair back. I felt really bad the next morning, though, like I was a bad friend. But seeing her act so helpless was a major trigger for me that brought back too many memories of my mom acting the same way.

Amanda's fling with my roommate didn't last very long. I kept noticing that he was spending an awful lot of time chatting on Facebook. It's not that I was spying, but it was hard not to notice, even from across the room, that whoever this other girl was, she was sending him nude photos of herself. I didn't want Amanda to get hurt. Just like in high school, we had each other's backs, and I wasn't about to let the scumbag screw her over. At the same time, I also didn't want to be the one who openly ratted him out. It could make our living situation pretty awkward. So I started dropping subtle (quickly followed by very obvious) hints to Amanda about how he spent so much time talking to people on Facebook, and she eventually got curious enough to sneak a peek at his computer. She ended the fling immediately, and since it had been going on for only a few weeks, no one was too devastated. Even better, I no longer had to hear them going at it every night.

Chloe and Amanda continued to go out and get drunk a couple of nights a week, and I started staying in more to work on WSP videos, since I was still traveling home each weekend to film new ones with Brittany. By that point, we had enough subscribers that we were earning close to one thousand dollars a month on ads, so I was taking our channel more seriously than ever before. But Amanda and Chloe started giving me a lot of crap for not going out with them. "Come on, Joey," Chloe would say. "Enjoy your college life!"

But I enjoyed my YouTube life more, and they started getting on my case about it. One night they were trying to get me to go out while I was in the middle of editing a video parody of Justin Bieber's song "One Time." We had reworked all of the lyrics so that it was about the game *Farmville* and got other YouTubers like iJustine to film parts for it too. It was silly, but I knew that, and I was really proud of the video.

"Joey, turn off your computer already and come out with us," Chloe whined.

"I've got to get this video finished. Here, watch this clip!" I played them a little bit of me lip-synching to the new lyrics while acting like Bieber. I smiled, waiting for them to start laughing, but Amanda didn't even look at the computer and stared intently at her phone instead.

That hurt. Amanda was one of my closest friends from high school. She had even been in a bunch of WSP videos, but she was suddenly acting as if she was too cool for them now in order to suck up to Chloe, who had never been that interested in them. I was confused by this sudden shift in our relationship. I wondered if she was embarrassed by me, or if maybe she was just trying to give me some sort of tough love about the video. Maybe it *did* suck and she just didn't want to say it out loud. I also think that I was a little jealous about how much she was bonding with Chloe. I felt that I was being excluded. (I was vindicated in the end. The video went viral after we posted it and now has over 10 million views.)

But the end result of that night was that nothing was ever the same between us. Chloe and Amanda started to hang out alone more and not include me, and when we did get together, Chloe constantly pointed out that she didn't think I was very smart. If I didn't know about a subject she was talking about or if I mispronounced a word, she'd call me out on it. She'd do it in a joking voice, but in a way that I could tell there was some genuine malice underneath. It made me start believing less and less in myself.

I didn't want to be totally friendless, though, so I put up with them, and one night they finally persuaded me to go with them to a party.

"It's going to be amazing," Chloe said. "You can't miss this one. I refuse to let you."

"Fine," I said with a sigh, and before I knew it, I was standing in yet another gross apartment surrounded by all the usual drunk frat boys.

"I'm not really comfortable here," I told Amanda.

"I don't care. Just relax, get a drink," she said. "Come on, Chloe, let's go find some boys."

I stood in a corner, totally miserable until out of nowhere, a familiar face appeared. It was a girl named Shanisa whom I'd casually known since the second grade. We had ridden the same bus together for a while, and we had even had a few of the same classes when we were older. Maybe I was about to make a new friend.

"Hi!" I said excitedly. "You know, I thought I recognized you on campus the other day. That's so cool that you go here too!"

"Yeah," she said, sort of listlessly. "So you're gay, right?"

"No," I stammered. "Who told you that?"

"Oh, no one. I just thought you were. My bad." She took a sip of her drink. "But are you sure, though?"

RUDE! I couldn't figure out where her question even came from, much less how it was appropriate to ask someone you barely knew. And here I'd thought that one time I'd let her sit next to me on the bus in second grade meant something. *What a bitch*, I thought as I turned away from her, but suddenly I got nervous. Was that still how people saw me? I'd thought I'd left that persona behind in high school. Maybe I should have kept making my voice sound deeper after all.

I was done with the party, and right then Amanda and Chloe showed up.

"Ugh, there are *no* cute boys here. Let's go to Randy's party," Chloe said.

So we trekked a few blocks over to another house party that was exactly like the one we had just left. There was a repeat of what happened at the last place, with me standing in the corner while they searched for boys to talk to. Chloe finally came to get me.

"This place sucks. Let's go back to the other party."

At this point, the two of them were fairly drunk, and I had had enough. I told them that I was going to go home instead. We got to an intersection at a main road where I could turn back to school and they could head to the other party.

"Okay, bye," I said. "Have fun!"

They stopped dead in their tracks. "Are you freaking kidding me?" Chloe asked.

Amanda joined in. "You're just going to leave us here? Two girls alone?"

I was dumbfounded. "I told you I was leaving. And besides, you guys wouldn't even talk to me at either of those parties."

"It's not our fault that you're so socially awkward, Joey," Chloe said.

"I'm just not having fun," I said. "But you guys go on without me."

"Wow, what a man," Chloe said with a sneer. "Leaving us here all alone in the street."

I looked around. There were tons of kids from the college wandering the sidewalks, party hopping.

"You guys go out all the time without me," I said. "You've never said anything about not feeling safe!"

"You're just being a little bitch!" Chloe screamed.

That was the last straw. I turned around and walked back to campus. I could still hear them screaming about what a coward I was from a block away.

I was so furious that I called Brittany as soon I got back to my room and told her what had happened. She felt bad for me but couldn't come over and comfort me because she lived so far away. I called my sister next. "I don't think I can take this anymore," I said, on the verge of tears. "I've had it. They are so mean to me!"

"You don't need that in your life," Nicole said. "Do you want me to come pick you up?" She was in college too at the time and wasn't as far away as Brittany.

I glanced at my computer screen and saw that Amanda had just logged on to AIM.

"No, that's okay. Thanks for listening. I love you," I said. Just hearing Nicole's voice had managed to calm me down. Once I hung up with her, I started typing a message to Amanda:

Joey: I'm not going to take any more shit from you two from here on out. You've been treating me like I'm an idiot all the time just because Chloe does.

Amanda: I'm pissed as hell, Joey. You don't leave two girls out alone at night.

Joey: You were both being so mean!

Amanda: What, because I told you for the millionth time to get off YouTube and come hang with us?

Joey: No, it's that whenever I say something, you don't care. Tonight you literally said, "I don't care."

Amanda: Whatever. I still can't believe you left us. You are so selfish. What kind of guy does that?

Joey: Amanda, you were fine. There were tons of people out.

Amanda: I know, but you don't know what could have happened.

Joey: You were like four houses away! Big whoop.

Amanda: You are such a dick. You never do anything anymore. All you do is sit at your stupid computer all day.

Joey: Speaking of, how about when I show you something I'm proud of, like my video, and you ignore it? Do you know how much that hurts?

Amanda: Well, I'm sorry, but I hate that stupid song. I don't care what the video is but anything with that song is shit. What do you want me to do? Sit there and tell you it was godly? You just sit at your lame computer, and you are a lazy piece of shit. Face it, you will never be anything in life and you will never get into Emerson.

I blocked her immediately and signed off AIM. I was shocked about how much hate she was spewing. I tried to keep things in perspective, knowing that she was drunk. Still, it was no excuse. She took it way too far—she knew how much getting into Emerson meant to me. As far as I was concerned, my friendship with both of them was over. I had a really brief text exchange with Chloe that was basically a rehash of the same conversation I had with Amanda.

The first few days without them were fine. I continued with my normal routine, and since I spent so much time working at my computer on WSP to begin with, I hardly noticed my sudden lack of friends. But after my fourth solo trip to the dining hall, I began to get depressed. Fitchburg was already cliquey to begin with, and now that we were a couple of months into the semester, none of them were taking applications for new members. I became a lone sailor and started to eat my feelings. I had the same meal day in and day out. I'd slink over to a table in the corner, sit by myself, and scarf down my dinner—a hamburger, a hot dog, a cherry Coke, and a vanilla/chocolate swirl ice-cream cone for dessert—as fast as I could and then race back to my dorm room.

I quickly got sick of eating alone in public, though, and eventually gave up on the dining hall. I'd get pizza delivered to my room or eat a bowl of cereal rather than have to face another lonely meal in front of a roomful of friends laughing with each other. I didn't have any classes on Fridays, so every

Thursday night my dad would pick me up and bring me back home so Brittany and I could work on more videos.

My mom had started drinking again, but because I wasn't living with her full-time, I tried to turn the other way and pretend nothing was happening. But it was hard because I worried so much that Jett might be experiencing some of the same things that I had experienced with her. And I suddenly started to wonder why no one in my family ever did anything to help get me out of the situation. Living with an alcoholic was certainly not easy, and it's not that people hadn't known what was going on. I had felt trapped.

My mom was like Dr. Jekyll and Mr. Hyde—there were two sides to her. I never stopped loving her, even when she was at her worst, because I still craved the moments when she was good. I just had to wait for her to sober up and get back to her nice self. It was an extremely unhealthy relationship. I knew that Jett was getting the good parts of our mom, but I was so scared of him ever having to deal with the bad parts too that I ended up having a conversation with Bob, asking him to make sure that Jett was being well taken care of. He assured me that he was, and I felt a little better.

I always dreaded having to return to school on Sunday nights and face another lonely week. I felt that I was living a double life. Online, I had friends across the world, and it seemed that my life was so fun when looked at through the lens of WinterSpringPro—full of dancing and laughing and collaborations with friends. But in real life it was the exact opposite.

I finally got so lonely that I called my sister and asked her how to make friends. "You just have to go out and meet people," she said. "Is there anyone at all that you're even talking to right now?"

JOEY GRACEFFA

There was one person—a guy named Todd from one of my film classes who seemed pretty cool. He had a YouTube channel of his own, and he'd stopped to talk to me a few times after our class together to ask questions about how to promote his videos. I'd give him some advice, but then he always rushed off before we could start up any sort of conversation. Whenever I'd see him around campus, he was always surrounded by a huge group of friends, so I never felt brave enough to approach him and try to develop a real friendship. But after talking to my sister, I screwed up all my courage and walked up to him after class one day.

"Hey, do you want to go to the gym sometime?"

"Huh?"

"You know, go work out. We could be, um, workout partners." *Workout partners?* I could feel myself blushing. This sounded ridiculous. It was like I was asking him out on a date.

"Sure, whatever," he said.

"Cool! How's tomorrow, at, like, four o'clock?"

He shrugged and finished gathering up his things. "That should work. Give me your number just in case," he said. We exchanged info and he wandered off.

I was elated. I'd never been to the campus gym before, but figured it couldn't hurt to start working out after all the junk food I'd been eating. The next afternoon I put on a pair of blue Abercrombie shorts and some cheap running shoes from Payless and walked across the quad, south of the main campus, and down to North Street.

The recreation center is a huge, windowless brick structure and looks more like a prison than a place to get healthy. It was early November by this point and freezing cold, but I didn't want to hang out in the lobby by myself, so I waited outside on a ramp, jumping up and down to try and keep myself warm.

I'm here, I texted at 4:05.

Outside, I mean, I texted at 4:12. *Are you already inside?*

Ten minutes later: *Did something come up?*

I finally gave up on him at 4:35 and rushed back to my dorm, diving under the covers to warm up my freezing legs.

When I saw him again in class the next day, I asked what had happened. "Oh, yeah, something came up. Sorry." He didn't offer to try again, so I gave up on him. But I wasn't ready to abandon my search for friends yet. I scanned the school's bulletin boards in search of activities that might be fun and saw that auditions were being held for a play. But the day I saw the flier was also the last day the auditions were being held, so I rushed straight to the auditorium. There was a girl sitting at a table in the lobby and she pointed to a sign-in sheet.

"You got here just in time," she whispered. "There's someone else in there reading now, and we thought he was going to be the last one for the day."

She handed me a copy of the script. "You should have some time to look this over before you're up."

I thanked her and scanned the printout, but it was a play I'd never heard of, and I wondered if a student had written it. I began to concentrate on the highlighted lines when the girl called my name. "Actually, you're up now after all," she said. "You can go on in."

I went inside and walked down the aisle toward the stage. An upperclassman was sitting in the third row with his feet up on the seat in front of him, and two other guys holding clipboards flanked him.

"Hi," I waved.

They nodded at me, and I walked up onto the stage and stood across from another guy holding the script.

"I'll read the other parts," he said. "Start whenever you're ready."

I hadn't had a chance to see more than three lines of dialogue before being called in, and so as you might imagine, the audition was a disaster. I stumbled over every other word. And since I didn't know what the scene was even about, I had no idea how I was supposed to be acting. The dialogue was pretty ambiguous—the character could have been happy or angry. It was impossible to tell. About halfway through the scene, I realized that I hadn't even looked up from the script once, so I quickly made eye contact with the other actor, who was staring at me like I was insane. I dropped my eyes back down to the page but lost my place and stood there saying "um, um, um" over and over until I found it again.

Once the ordeal was finally, mercifully over, the director called out "Thank you," with disdain practically dripping out of his mouth.

I didn't even bother checking the callback sheets the following day. Maybe I was actually cast in the lead role and just never found out. But somehow I doubt that.

The one thing that kept me from going absolutely out of my mind was—you guessed it—YouTube. I had started to become closer and closer to my online friends, like a girl named Meghan who ran a channel called Strawburry 17. I became a little obsessed with her. Every morning I'd wake up, eat a bowl of Apple Cinnamon Cheerios, and watch her new daily vlog. She'd chat about her cool life and take viewers along with her on little adventures, and she'd sometimes really open up about her personal life. Her mom had some issues with prescription drugs, and her childhood wasn't the greatest. I was shocked: I didn't think anyone else was going through anything remotely similar to what I had been through. It was cool to see someone I admired so much being open and vulnerable about her personal life. I didn't talk about my family issues with anyone. Literally, no one. I couldn't imagine how she had the guts to expose that sort of information to the world. (Little did I know that one day I'd write an entire book about my personal life.)

Anyway, I'd pretend that I was hanging out with her when I watched her videos, and she made me feel that I was catching up with an old friend every day. I eventually reached out to her online to tell her how much I liked her work, and we began writing back and forth and then video chatting. I developed a little crush on her. She was cute and funny and smart, but she was also located all the way across the country, so there wasn't much I could do about it.

Winter break was approaching, and it couldn't come fast enough. After Amanda had broken up with the stoner, he had started going to fewer and fewer classes, until he stopped going completely. He was in the room constantly, smoking pot and playing *Grand Theft Auto*. I never had any time to myself, but I also never felt so alone. We lived together with our headphones on—him lost in video games and me meticulously editing videos. When we did talk, I'd try to persuade him to go to class. (Okay, maybe it was more out of a desire to finally have some alone time.) He never listened though, and by the end of the semester he was expelled, which meant I'd have the whole room all to myself when we got back from break. But that was the only good thing I could see about returning to college after the holidays.

Five Essential Items to Bring to College

1. Flip-flops to wear in the gross, grimy shower.

2. A shower caddy so no one steals your conditioner.

3. Stuff to decorate your room with that makes you feel safe and reminds you of home.

4. At least two pairs of sheets, because with everything else going on, your laundry probably won't get done that often.

5. Your true self. If you try to be someone you're not, you're just going to end up attracting the wrong kinds of friends.

How to Get Along with Your First College Roommate

1. Be open to your roommate's interests and the stuff that he or she does. The chances of your getting a roomie who is exactly like you is zero.

2. Be willing to share space. If you have some

sort of invisible line in your head dividing the room, you're setting yourself up for failure. Your roommate's coffee mug <u>will</u> accidentally end up on your desk at some point, and it's no big deal.

3. Be respectful about food. Don't eat things that don't belong to you, but if you do, let your roomie know immediately and replace the item within twenty-four hours.

4. Share your class schedules so you each know when you'll have alone time in the room.

5. If you truly can't stand each other, rally for a room change before the bad situation really escalates.

How to Tell If You're in a Toxic Friendship

It's weird how often people end up being friends with someone who is terrible for their self-esteem. But a lot of times people stay in the friendship because they've been in it so long that they don't even realize that something is wrong. Here are a few signs that it might be time to friend-dump someone:

1. You feel down about yourself after you hang out with the person.

2. You feel that you are always trying to win the person's affection.

3. He or she is controlling you in some way (a classic example is telling you that you shouldn't hang out with certain other people).

4. You only ever get to do things that your friend wants to do, not what you want to do.

How to Get Out of a Toxic Friendship

Friend-dumping someone doesn't have to be dramatic. A slow fadeout is usually better than a big screaming match. Just take a few steps back from the relationship, then a few more, and usually by that point the person should get the hint. If not, then it's necessary to have a real conversation so things don't get any worse. My advice is to just gently say that you feel that you have different interests from this person and that you want to pursue them.

How to Pick the Right College for You

Do your research. Start with location—if you're a city person, go to a big city, but if you're not, don't force yourself because you'll be miserable. Once you've figured that out, think about your interests, and find schools that have strong departments for what you think you want to major in (and remember that you don't have to pick a major before you begin college; you can always switch, so be sure to check out the different disciplines offered). Research the alumni, and see what they have accomplished. Once you've picked out a few colleges you like, be sure to apply to a few backups just in case.

How to Deal with College Rejection Letters

Everything happens for a reason. Either push yourself to work harder so you can reapply and transfer, or have a good cry and move on. Your ideal college might have been full of snobby, pretentious people and your backup college could be the place where you meet the love of your life. You just really never know. If Emerson hadn't rejected me, I would never have ended up where I am today, and I wouldn't change that for anything.

Chapter 9

Not-So-Happy New Year

My winter break was three weeks long, and I couldn't wait to have a bedroom and bathroom all to myself and work with Brittany on more videos. But it became pretty clear after I got back that my mom was in really bad shape. She and Bob had technically split up (AGAIN), but he was still living in the house so he could take care of Jett. Thank god, because she was drunk almost every night. But every damn morning it would be like nothing had happened. We were all so used to her being sloshed by that point that her behavior became the norm. It was all so depressing, and I tried to get out of the house as much as possible. Brittany and I worked on some WSP projects, including a video parody of Lady Gaga's "Monster." We changed all the lyrics to fit *The Jersey Shore* and Brittany dressed up as Snookie. We used tons of self-tanning powder to make her face as orange as possible. It was hilarious and so much fun to make.

On New Year's Eve, I just wanted to have a quiet night at home with friends and watch movies. After such a terrible first semester at college, I needed a low-key and drama-free evening to usher in 2010. I invited Brittany, my cousin Justin, and two other friends from high school, Hannah and Mariah, over to my house for a sleepover. Hannah and Mariah are great, and if you watch old WSP videos, you'll see them pop up from time to time. They are lighthearted and freaking funny, and they taught me to laugh difficult situations off if there was nothing else I could do. Anyone else might freak out if someone hacked their Facebook account and posted, "Ugh, I'm pregnant AGAIN," on their home page, but Hannah thought pranks like that were hysterical, even when they happened to her.

Our plan for the night was to watch an utterly bizarre horror film from the nineties, *The People under the Stairs*. It's about a psychotic brother-and-sister couple who give birth to a bunch of cannibal kids they keep in their basement. In theory, it should be totally creepy, but the film is ridiculous and campy and a total trip. We made popcorn and settled in for the night. Just before the movie began, my mom told me that she was going to The 99, a restaurant a few blocks away that she frequented. It also had a bar. I knew that she'd come stumbling home drunk at some point, but hoped that it wouldn't happen until after everyone had already gone to sleep.

No such luck.

Just as the movie was ending, the front door swung open. My mom and a strange guy were standing on our front steps.

"Hi, Joey! This is Max. He made sure I got home from The 99 safe, and he also brought some beers for you and your friends! Don't worry, he used to be a police officer. Shhhhh, don't tell!"

The guy was tall and skinny and wearing a black leather jacket. "Yeah, they're out here if you want them," he said.

All I could think was, *Eww, who is this crusty man coming to my party to give my friends and me booze?* None of us drank. He dropped the grocery bag of beer on the steps, but I didn't make a move to get them. I was so frustrated and suddenly just snapped. "Who the hell are you?" I asked. "You can leave now."

He laughed it off while my mom said, "Be nice, Joey."

110

This was embarrassing. As far as my friends knew, my mom and Bob were still together. He in fact was asleep in the house at that very moment! So who was this random dude my mom was hanging with outside in the freezing cold? I ran upstairs to Bob's room and told him what was going on.

"You need to come downstairs. Mom brought some weird guy home," I said.

I heard him mutter something under his breath as he stepped out into the hallway.

"Can you get rid of him?" I asked. "It's creeping me out." Not to mention that I was appalled that my friends had to see my mom in this condition.

"I'll take care of it," he said.

He went downstairs and walked outside. Thankfully Officer Max didn't put up any sort of struggle and wandered off into the night.

I turned to my friends. "Sooo, what do you guys want to watch next?" I asked.

They could tell I was humiliated, but they all just laughed the situation off and pretended that there was nothing weird at all about my mother bringing home a cop who wanted to get us drunk.

Bob went back upstairs, but my mom had no intention of letting the party end. "Come on kids, let's daaance!" she said, swaying her hips to imaginary music. "It's New Year's Eve! Let's parteeeeee! Whooooo!" Mom sat down on Brittany's lap, who looked horrified. "Come on darling, you'll dance with me, right?"

"MOM! GO TO BED!" I yelled.

Hannah and Mariah could tell how mortified I was and started doing everything they could to defuse the situation by playing along with my mom, laughing and joking and dancing around with her. I loved them so much in that moment. But I finally had enough when Mom lowered her voice and asked, "Do any of you want a drink? It's a special night!"

"Stop trying to be the mom from *Mean Girls*," I said with a groan. "Please, just go to bed."

She finally left, but she acted all wounded. "Don't be rude," she pouted. "I'm your mother!" She stomped up the stairs and I heard her bedroom door slam.

We called it a night too, and the next morning we all pretended that nothing had happened. I managed to avoid Mom the next day, which was also my plan for the rest of winter break. I tried to be out of the house whenever I knew she would be around, but we kept crossing paths. I'd come home and find her crying at the kitchen table with a glass half full of wine or a Coors Lite in front of her, and I had zero sympathy. I was fed up. "Stop crying," I'd tell her. "You're being a brat." I didn't care if I sounded mean or hurt her. I *wanted* to hurt her, because once more, she was destroying our relationship.

One night when I was getting ready to go to bed, I found her sitting on the stairs with a cup in her hand, blocking my way.

"Excuse me," I said. She didn't budge.

"You have no idea what I have to put up with," she said.

"Yeah? Like what?" I said.

"I have to clean up after you, I have to take care of Jett, and Bob treats me like crap. All I do is work."

"We all work, Mom," I said. "Stop acting like a child and be an adult for once."

"You don't do anything!" she screamed, standing up to face me. "You're just a lazy, rude, ungrateful child!"

"Okay, whatever. You're a pathetic drunk who can't even take care of her kids," I said. I felt horrible as soon as the words came out of my mouth. It was one thing to be embarrassed by my mom and tell her to stop drinking in front of my friends, but it was another to outright insult her like that. She spun around and I saw pure rage in her eyes. She slammed me up against the wall, pinning my wrists with her hands.

"Don't you ever talk to me like that!" she screamed, spitting in my face. "You are a clueless little . . ."

I didn't let her finish the sentence. I managed to wrench free of her hands, grab hold of her wrists, and push her off me hard. She stumbled back but didn't fall, and I felt a sudden wave of shame and regret course through me. *I just pushed my mother*, I thought. Her eyes were wide open in shock as she regained her balance and I fled up the stairs to my room before anything else could happen. I locked the door behind me and threw myself on the bed, willing myself not to cry, but it didn't work. I was filled with anger and guilt and had no idea how to get rid of it. I could hear her fumbling around and cursing downstairs, so I pulled a pillow over my head, trying to drown out the sounds of her crying and yelling, "No one cares about me!"

Hearing your mother cry is one of the hardest things in the world, even if she's just drunk. I wanted to go and comfort her, but at the same time I felt that she didn't *deserve* to be comforted, so I swallowed all of my sympathy. *Good, let her cry*, I thought. Brick by brick a huge wall was going up between us, and I was starting to no longer even see her as my mother.

The New Year was off to a disastrous start, but I was determined to turn it around. I knew I couldn't keep living like that—miserable at both home and school. Something needed to change.

Violence Is Never the Answer

To this day, I'm horrified that I pushed my mom during our fight. I know that it was a heat-of-the-moment thing, but I wish I'd had more self-control. If you're in the middle of an argument and you can feel it escalating to the point where you want to push or shove or even hit the other person, take a deep breath and walk away. Winning a verbal fight isn't worth the damage you can cause if it's getting you so worked up that you might strike someone. Go to your room, punch the mattress, and wait for the feelings to pass. Never be the one to take an argument to a physical place.

New Year's Eve Resolutions

A lot of people promise a lot of crap on New Year's Eve, only to promptly forget all about whatever it was they said the next day. And you know what? That's just fine. It's part of the

American tradition. But if you're really looking to make a big change in your life, New Year's Eve can be a great milestone marker to use for charting progress. So instead of getting drunk, blurting out that you're going to exercise more, and then spending New Year's Day hungover and eating nachos on the couch, take New Year's Eve as a time to write out a set of goals for yourself. Hang them up next to your bed or your desk so that you're constantly reminded throughout the year of the objectives you've set for yourself.

Chapter 10

The Road to Recovery

Once I was back at school, having a dorm room all to myself was both a blessing and a curse. On the one hand, I had a place where I could be alone. On the other hand, I was alone ALL OF THE TIME. I still had no friends. Amanda had ended up transferring to another school, but Chloe was still around. Dreading the thought of another semester of eating solo, I sucked up my pride and apologized to her about the night I left her and Amanda after the party.

I just don't want things to be weird between us anymore, I texted her.

Chloe accepted my apology (even though I still didn't think I'd done anything wrong), but she also made me work really hard to get her friendship back. As a sort of punishment, I always had to escort her back to her dorm room anytime we hung out. I needed to be her little bodyguard. It was exhausting, and luckily she kept me on a leash only for the first couple of weeks before she finally loosened her grip. Socially, things eased up for me. I managed to make a few other friends. But I still hated being there. It didn't feel like the right place for me. I felt like I was just treading water.

I doubt it was just coincidence that Chloe started being nice to me around the time of one of WSP's biggest successes up to that point. Toward the end of January, Brittany and I posted a video of Lady Gaga's "Bad Romance" done entirely in beat box style. YouTube ended up featuring it on its home page a few days later, along with three other videos from other users. Lady Gaga saw ours and tweeted about it, and WinterSpring-Pro exploded. We got around 20,000 subscribers in that one day alone.

I knew that I was doing something right with my life. Chloe had to give me some begrudging respect since all the time I spent in front of my computer was amounting to something. She didn't bug me as much after that about not wanting to go out to parties, but she wasn't partying as much either.

Since my plan was still to try and transfer to Emerson, I threw myself into my film classes. The only problem was that none of my previous experience making videos got me anywhere with my teacher. We were allowed to use only one kind of camera that was confusing to work with, and the final images looked awful. Worse, we were required to use an antiquated editing system, which was way more complicated than it needed to be. I'd learned how to use Adobe Premiere Elements when I was just fifteen, and I hated that I wasn't allowed to use my own software. The process for checking out a school-owned camera to use for our homework assignments took forever, and trying to return it was just as tedious. Plus, my own camera was of a much better quality.

There were also severe restrictions on the types of things we had to film: assignments had to be shot exactly as the teacher wanted, and they didn't allow any room for creativity. Everything was just about setting up camera shots, getting wide angles or mediums or close-ups. There was no focus on the story, and stories were what I was interested in. Everything I was making on YouTube was way more fun. When I tried to talk to the teacher about it, he dismissed me; he didn't want to hear about anything we had worked on in the past. To him we were all just stupid teenagers who didn't know anything about film.

Our big final project at the end of the semester was to shoot a documentary. I chose to do mine on a company I worked for during a summer in high school. Juniper Farms is a sixty-five year-old family-run company that specializes in home heating oil services and ice-cream delivery. Random, I know. But since I had a relationship with it, I knew I'd have lots of access and interview time. I hated the school camera and editing equipment so much that I ended up using my own instead. I figured I could export the final product to the school's editing software system. It didn't work, and the teacher knocked an entire grade off my final project so that I got a B instead of an A.

I did have an English teacher who was incredibly supportive of my video work, though, and she cheered me on in my decision to reapply to Emerson. For certain assignments, she would let me create short films instead of writing papers. For example, we were supposed to write a paper on someone we considered a hero, and she let me turn in a music video I made about my sister Nicole. The video ended up being really morbid. It was a montage of me in a graveyard crying, cut with videos of us as kids, and then us getting into a car crash where she died but I survived. The class was totally silent after I played it. I think they were all really weirded out, and everyone thought my sister was dead. Even my teacher was freaked, but she still ended up writing me a glowing recommendation letter for my reapplication to Emerson, and I submitted a new five-minute film. I stuck with the horror theme, but I tried to make it more noir and spookier instead of an outright slasher film. It was about a boy being haunted by a mysterious ghost-like stranger who made him sleepwalk. I called it "Evil Insomniac."

I ended up getting wait-listed. It was incredibly frustrating. I felt that I was so close to my dream, and now it was dangling just out of reach.

I was still going home on the weekends but continued to avoid my mom as much as possible. We never discussed what had happened over winter break, but it's not like there was ever a chance. She was still drunk a lot of the time, but Bob finally persuaded her to go to rehab. Again.

I know it sounds cold, but I had finally hit the point where I lost all respect for her. Our relationship was broken, and I didn't see the warrior in her anymore. She'd become a helpless person who sucked the energy out of life, and I wanted no part of it. The wall of self-protection that I'd been building was finally completed. I didn't trust that she had any intention of getting better. She had started and stopped drinking so many times by that point that I didn't see what sort of difference another trip to rehab could make.

She went in for another thirty-day program, and after about two weeks I got a message from Bob letting me know that the center was hosting a family day, where the patients could be reunited with their loved ones in a big group setting. I had no interest in seeing her until she had at least a month of sobriety under her belt, but Bob insisted that showing our support was an important part of her recovery. And that is how, one warm spring Saturday afternoon, I ended up at a state park located a few towns over from Marlborough with a bunch of recovering addicts and their families.

I saw Mom sitting at a picnic table as soon as we got out of the car. She looked healthier, with some color in her cheeks and the dark circles under her eyes gone. I had a sudden spark of hope that this would be the last time she'd be in rehab. But I also felt that I needed to protect myself from getting my expectations destroyed. My emotions kept swinging back and forth between not believing in her and telling myself not to give up hope, that it was just a matter of time before she got better for good. My sister and little brother were there as well, and since I was so torn between my emotions, I let them do most of the talking, choosing instead to hang back. And after studying the crowd, I suddenly wanted to leave. I was uncomfortable around the other families and their junkie relatives. Watching all the tearful reunions happening around me was too raw, and I still wasn't ready to forgive my mother. My jumbled thoughts kept swirling: I didn't have any sympathy for her situation, but I also felt incredibly guilty for not having any sympathy.

"I'm so glad you came, Joey," she told me. "I want to introduce you to some of the friends I've made."

The last thing I wanted to do was meet the other alcoholics my mom was hanging out with. I was scared that instead of attending AA meetings together when they got out, I'd just end up seeing them all together at my mom's kitchen table chugging beer.

I think I lasted about ten minutes before I told my mom that I wasn't feeling well and was going to sit in the car. She looked disappointed, and I tried to avoid eye contact as I gave her a quick hug good-bye. I ran off before anyone could stop me. I slumped down in the backseat of Bob's car as far as I could. More than anything else, I just wished my mom could be normal.

Another complication was that I had started experimenting with drinking myself, the way most other freshmen in college do. Was this where I was headed? I didn't think so. The few times I'd had a couple of mixed drinks, I'd felt all warm and fuzzy, but never mean or out of control. With my mom, it was like alcohol flipped a switch inside her and turned her into a completely different person. If I felt myself starting to get a little messy, there was always a part of me that made me stop. I couldn't understand why my mother wasn't the same way. I understand now that alcoholism is a disease, and I know how lucky I am not to have it. Especially since now that I'm over twenty-one, it's fun to go out to a bar with friends. But I still have very little tolerance for people who insist on going out drinking and getting out of control.

When my family finally got back to the car, I asked how the rest of the visit had been.

"Really good," said Bob. "She wished you had stayed longer but she understands why you didn't. Recovery takes a long time."

He wasn't kidding. Mom was back at home a few weeks later and seemed fine. In fact, for about six months everything kept getting better and better. She returned to her old self, laughing and joking and being supportive and interested in what was going on in my life. I watched her interact with Jett, now three years old, the same way she had taken care of me when he was my age, swinging him around in her arms and singing. All the love that had been suppressed by the alcohol came right back to the surface, and she spread her joy around our whole family. It felt too good to be true.

And, sadly, it was. That half-year was amazing, but out of nowhere she went back to drinking. I think this is a battle she will always be fighting. All I can do is be there for her as much as possible. Our relationship has gotten much stronger over the years. I can forgive her for a lot of what happened. I've also learned to not be ashamed of who she is. When I first started talking about her on YouTube, I was amazed at how much support I got, as well as how many other kids have had similar— or much worse—experiences. If I can talk openly about her, maybe it will help other kids with alcoholic parents feel a little less alone. My relationship with Mom continues to be off and on, but even during the off periods, I still hold on to that image I had of her as a child—the warrior woman, the mom who danced with me and encouraged all of my imaginary games. I now know that person will always be inside her.

Alcoholism Is a Disease

Alcoholism is a chronic disease, which means it will last a lifetime. Luckily, it can also be kept under control through treatment. The problem is that the alcoholic has to <u>want</u> to get better, and that's usually the biggest hurdle to overcome. My mom has been in and out of rehab many times, and each time she's been released I've hoped it would be the time that sobriety would stick. So far it hasn't, but even if there ever does come a year, two, or even five that she remains sober, it's something she will struggle with her whole life. Staying better will require constant diligence with the help of resources like AA meetings, therapy, and lots and lots of communication with family and friends.

Some Sobering Statistics

If you live with an alcoholic parent and feel that you're alone in the world, here are some figures from the National Institute on Alcohol Abuse and Alcoholism that will help put your position into a larger perspective:

♦ Ten percent of American children live with a parent who has a problem with alcohol.

♦ According to the most recent study, 17 million adults have some sort of alcohol use disorder.

♦ Nearly 88,000 people die annually from alcohol—related causes. It's the third—largest preventable cause of death in the United States.

On Forgiveness

No matter what my mom puts me through, I will always forgive her. Forgiving someone for his or her mistakes is probably one of the most important things you can do in your lifetime, and it will make you a better, happier person. These three people summed it up better than I ever could:

"The weak can never forgive. Forgiveness is the attribute of the strong." —Gandhi

"Forgiveness is not an occasional act, it is a constant attitude." —Martin Luther King Jr.

"True forgiveness is when you can say, 'Thank you for that experience.'" —Oprah Winfrey

Chapter 11

California, Here We Come

At the end of my freshman year, Emerson officially re-jected me. Again. The only thing that kept me from spiraling into a deep depression was my decision to travel with Brittany to the very first VidCon, a conference in Southern California that was sort of modeled after Comic-Con, only it was billed for "People Who Love Online Media." That was us. A lot of our online friends, like iJustine and Shane Dawson, were going to be there, so we booked a flight to go and join them. Even better, Meghan, my online crush, was going to be there too. She needed a place to stay, so we decided that she would crash with us.

It was Brittany's first time ever on an airplane and she was sort of freaked out. She didn't want to go anywhere near the window and kept her eyes squeezed shut during take-off. We recognized a few other YouTubers at the Boston airport, but no one we knew personally. They were mostly the kids who posted videos about blowing different things up in micro-waves (not that I was in any position to judge!).

I couldn't wait to get to Los Angeles. I'd never been there before, so we decided to stay an extra two days after the con-ference to explore the city. I pictured palm trees, an endless blue sky, and a steady, perfect 73 degree air temperature. What we got instead was nonstop rain. The city seemed gloomy and depressing, not at all like the glamorous paradise

I'd envisioned. Everything seemed really dirty and ugly, just an endless stream of strip malls. Still, we were too psyched to let anything get to us. We'd booked a room at the Hyatt Regency at Century Plaza, where the convention was taking place. I was hoping that we might get to meet a few of our fans, but nothing prepared for me for the first group of girls who started screaming our names as we walked through the lobby to check into our rooms.

"We love you!" they kept shouting and squealing before asking Brittany and me for autographs.

"Did that just actually happen?" I asked her once they left and we made it into the elevator.

"That was so cool," she said. "It's too weird!"

We met up with Meghan after we checked in and showed her to our room. It was so bizarre to finally meet this girl whom I felt so close to for so long for the first time in the flesh. I gave her a huge hug hello and was surprised at how tiny she was under her baggy hoodie. Her almond-shaped eyes peered out from under her bangs, making her look like a little woodland pixie. I still had feelings for her, but there wasn't any sort of physical spark. Emotionally, however, everything was great. It felt like reuniting with a childhood best friend.

Compared to what it's become now, VidCon was tiny that first year. There were a few scheduled autograph-signing sessions with bigger YouTubers like Smosh and Lisa Nova, along with a few sponsor booths. But for the most part, it consisted of a lot of walking around and meeting people, many of whom we'd had a lot of contact with but never in real life. It was always crazy when someone recognized us, but for the most part, it was us freaking out over seeing other YouTubers whom *we* were seeing in person for the first time. There was one in particular, a musician named Luke Conard, who ended up becoming a pretty big part of my life later.

We knew we wanted to approach iJustine since she'd appeared in two of our videos and I had become pretty friendly online. But she was still basically a celebrity to us, so we waited in a huge line for her meet-and-greet session. When it was our turn, she recognized us immediately.

"I love you guys!" she said. We chatted for a bit longer before we realized that we were holding up the line. But then she said that she wanted to chat with us some more and suggested that we all get coffee after VidCon.

Brittany and I exchanged glances. It was one thing to finally meet one of our idols, but to have her ask us out for coffee took it to a whole other level.

"That would be awesome," I said. "We're sticking around for a couple of extra days."

She gave us her number, and I think that's when everything started to really sink in. We weren't there just as fans; we were an actual part of this fast-growing community. We *belonged* there.

The moment that truly changed our lives forever, though, was meeting Lisa Nova. She was a major deal in the world of YouTube. Not only had she been the first YouTuber to cross over to mainstream television, as a cast member on *MADtv*, she was one of the cofounders of Maker Studios, a company based in Los Angeles where the biggest and best YouTubers got to meet up and collaborate on videos and cross-promote each other. We saw her chatting with a few people in the convention main hall, and I turned to Brittany. "We have to talk to her. No matter what."

"I know," she said. "Let's go lurk nearby until we get a chance."

So we did, and the second there was a lull in her conversation with the other group of people, we pounced. "WE LOVE YOU!" I said.

"Seriously, you're our favorite," Brittany said.

"WinterSpringPro!" she said, her eyes growing wide. "I love you guys too! Your videos are so funny!"

I just about died. I couldn't believe she even knew who we were, let alone thought our videos were good. We talked for a little longer before she had to rush off to a panel. "I'd love to get back in touch with you," she said before she left. "Can I get your e-mail?"

"Of course," I said, and entered it into her phone when she offered it to me.

"Awesome. I'm going to be in touch. I promise."

We figured it was just politeness, so it was a shock when I got an e-mail from her inviting us out to Maker Studios for a tour. Good thing we'd thought to tack a couple of extra days onto our trip.

When we got to Maker, I was surprised at how tiny the operation was. Back then the building was pretty small, with offices on the first floor and costume wardrobes on the second, so the tour didn't take very long.

"You could be a part of this, you know," Lisa said while we were there. "The two of you are so cute, and we'd love to work with you."

Again, it just seemed like something she was saying to be nice. We couldn't imagine that she would want to work with us. We seemed so rinky-dink compared to the people they were working with, like Shay Carl, a YouTube personality and comedian with five different channels and millions of fans whom he calls his "Shaytards." We played it off like, "Yeah, that would be cool someday." But we never dreamed it would actually happen.

We met up with iJustine later for coffee, and talking with her was like catching up with a long-lost friend. We all just clicked immediately.

Brittany was checking Twitter on her phone—probably getting ready to brag that we were hanging out with iJustine—when she saw a post that Fred was shooting a music video in the Valley. He listed the address so people could show up and act as extras.

"Should we go?" Justine asked. It made sense, since she had been a part of the video we had done when Fred reached 1 million subscribers.

"Let's do it!" I said.

We piled into her car and drove out to a Target parking lot in the middle of the suburbs. It was over 90 degrees that day, and we were all dripping with sweat. None of us really felt like dancing, but the idea of finally meeting Fred/Lucas in person seemed like an excellent cap to what had already been a perfect trip.

As we joined the throng of extras, Lucas walked by. He looked just as cute and baby-faced in person as he does when playing Fred. Justine called his name and he ran over, immediately recognizing her. Then his eyes wandered to us.

"Oh my god, it's WinterSpringPro!"

He had to rush off right afterward, but it didn't matter. He had recognized us. I couldn't imagine ever getting tired of that feeling. We danced our butts off in the boiling heat in front of the cameras for a few hours before heading to the airport.

Leaving Los Angeles was depressing. We'd been shown a world that we knew we belonged in. Once we got off the plane back in Boston, I had another e-mail waiting for me from Lisa, this one formally asking us if we'd be a part of Maker.

"Brittany, this is legit," I said. "We could do this for real. It could be our actual careers."

"This is insane," she said.

"You know what it means, though, right? We'd have to move to LA."

"Done," she said. "I've got nothing for me here." She was about as happy at her community college as I was at Fitchburg.

I realized that I didn't have anything on the East Coast for me either. I wasn't about to apply to Emerson for a third time, especially now that I was being offered a chance to jump into real life. Plus everyone we'd met at VidCon had been amazing. We had finally found our tribe—people who understand how absurdly fun it is to walk around with a camera everywhere and make silly videos, people who understand how exciting it is to make people laugh and connect with strangers from around the world. In Massachusetts, Brittany and I had been living in a bubble with WSP. Having friends like Meghan and iJustine online had been great, but now there was a chance to be friends with them out in the real world.

We e-mailed Maker Studios and told them that we were in. Bob hired a lawyer, and there were a couple of months of back-and-forth contract negotiations, and then it was done. During that time, the video we'd filmed with Fred premiered on Nickelodeon, and we saw ourselves in the background. We could officially say that we had been on television. It felt like a sign that we were making the right decision.

Brittany and I both officially dropped out of college and

began to make a plan. Surprisingly, our parents were cool with our decision. They'd seen how much effort we'd poured into our channel over the years, so it didn't seem that we were just chasing some random dream. We knew we needed to make another trip to Los Angeles to line up an apartment, but we decided to wait until January before making the actual move, so that we could save up enough money to keep us afloat for a while once we got there.

That fall we got an e-mail from Luke Conard, the musician we'd met at VidCon, and he invited us to a show he was playing in Boston. We went and had a blast, and he ended up asking us out to dinner with him and his friends after the concert. We all piled into their tour van, which is where I met Luke's roommates, Jason and Alex. They were the first people I'd ever met who loved *World of Warcraft* as much as I did, and it felt really cool to finally have some guy friends. We nerded out over the game for hours, and all I could think was, *How come I didn't have guy friends like this in high school?*

Brittany and I went back to Los Angeles that fall to look for an apartment to live in, and Luke offered to let us crash at his place for a few days.

"I made up the porch for you guys so you can have some privacy," he said when we arrived. I stayed in the living room and caught up with him while Brittany headed to the enclosed area outside with our bags. She came back right as Luke went into the kitchen to fix us something to eat. She was pale.

"We can't sleep in there," she whispered.

"Why not?" I whispered back.

"The bed is full of spiders!"

"WHAT?" I yelled and she shushed me, grabbed my arm, and pulled me out to the porch.

"Lift up the pillow," she said.

There were two of them, propped up on a dingy-looking mattress half-covered by a sheet. I gingerly lifted up one of the pillows, and, sure enough, about six big, hairy spiders went scurrying all over the place.

I jumped back quickly and looked at Brittany. "What the hell are we doing here?" We both started giggling uncontrollably at how absurd the situation was. We had almost no money, were planning on moving to the other side of the country to chase a dream that could possibly tank, and now we had to sleep in a spider bed.

We slept on the living room couches without any blankets. We didn't want to embarrass Luke, so we lied and told him it was because we didn't want to share a bed. We were both freezing all night and headed to Target the next day to pick up some new pillows and sleeping bags.

Meghan showed up in town a few days later to stay with Luke as well, to attend a party for a charity called Project for Awesome that was being hosted by John and Hank Green (John's the guy who wrote the movie *The Fault in Our Stars*; Hank runs cool science and ecology vlogs). Justine was there, and once she heard our spider story, she insisted that we pack our stuff and stay with her for the rest of the trip. She became our Los Angeles mentor and tour guide, but while we looked at a ton of apartments, nothing in our price range was remotely livable.

Finally, on our last day, we drove to Culver City to check out a development called The Meadows. The buildings circled a huge pool with a fountain at one end of it, and we saw an apartment that had a great layout, with a balcony and bedrooms on opposite ends of the space so we would have a lot of privacy. We'd even each get our own bathroom. Best of all, we could afford it as long as we stayed on a pretty strict budget. We signed a lease for January 2, and made it to the airport just in time to head home.

Tips on Being a Good Houseguest

1. Bring a small gift as a thank-you.
2. Clean up after yourself.
3. Offer to help with cooking.
4. If your friend has a dog, offer to take it for a walk.
5. Don't write about your host's spider-infested bed in a book. ;-)

My Favorite Spots in Los Angeles

The Getty Center. This huge museum is located on top of a big cliff that looks out over all of Los Angeles. You take an air tram up the side of the mountain to get there, and there are beautiful gardens all over the property. I always feel like I'm floating above the city when I visit.

Third Street Promenade. It's basically a big outdoor mall in Santa Monica. The shops are great, but I love people-watching there even more.

Runyan Canyon Park. Covering 160 acres, this park has loads of hiking trails for beginners and experts. Going there is like working out without actually realizing that you're working out.

Urth Caffé. This small chain is mostly known for its organic coffees, but trust me that the green tea-blended boba is where it's at. It might look like a McDonald's Shamrock Shake, but it's pure health and sunshine.

Whole Foods. I know these are everywhere in America, but I'd never been to one before moving to LA. Now I can't live without it. Whole Foods is where I do 99.9 percent of my grocery shopping.

Chapter 12

La-La Land

I had no idea how I was going to get all of my stuff to Los Angeles. I researched movers but quickly realized that it would be cheaper for me to just buy all new stuff, like a bed, once I got out there. I packed really light, just a couple of boxes. I liked the idea of bringing a small amount of stuff with me—it helped hammer home the idea in my mind that I was leaving my old life behind.

The plan was for us to leave around midnight so we could get a huge head start on the trip without hitting any traffic. Brittany arrived in her little blue Toyota Yaris, and I discovered that she had stuffed the car almost entirely with her own things.

"There's only room for one box!" I said as I peered into her cramped trunk.

"Sorry," she shrugged.

So I pared my possessions down even more, and my mom promised to mail the rest out to me. Since we were leaving so late at night, I'd already said good-bye to Jett before he'd gone to bed. I promised to be back to visit soon, and while I'm not sure if he fully understood what was happening, he hugged me extra tight. I tried not to feel too guilty. A part of me felt that I was abandoning him, but I knew Bob would be watching out for him.

When it came time to leave later that night, I hugged Mom and Bob good-bye. I tried hard to act carefree, but the truth was that I was terrified of leaving my family behind. As hard as everything had been, it was the only life I knew. I was positive that there was something bigger and better waiting for me out there in the world, but even that knowledge couldn't stop the feeling of vulnerability that came with moving so far away. And not only was I feeling scared about that, I felt responsible for my mom's well-being, even though I knew that leaving was probably the healthiest thing I could do for myself.

When we stopped by my dad's house to say good-bye to him and my sister, the level of emotion went into hyperdrive. I'd never once seen my dad cry before, but he had tears streaming down his face as he kissed my forehead. There's nothing more intense than seeing your father cry for the first time ever because he loves you so much.

"I'm so proud of you," he said. "Just promise me you'll be safe, and call me when you get there so I know you arrived in one piece."

Nicole was sobbing too. "I know you're going to kick butt out there," she sniffled. "But god, I wish it wasn't so far away."

"I'm going to be fine," I assured them, even though I had no idea if that was true. I managed to hold it together as we said our final good-byes, but as soon as we got back into the car, I started bawling my eyes out. Everything hit me at once: I was leaving home and everything I knew. I'd dropped out of college to take a chance on a dream that millions of other people have chased and failed at. It was a very focused awakening that I was entering a whole new chapter of my life. Even when we had gone out there to apartment hunt, it still hadn't felt completely real. But now everything felt crystal clear. Brittany let me finish crying it all out, and I recovered pretty quickly. I knew that I was strong enough to succeed.

That first night we drove for ten hours straight, switching turns at the wheel every three hours. We decided to take a southern route to avoid any potential snowstorms, and we didn't pull over to sleep until we had reached Virginia. We got up early and listened to Katy Perry's *Teenage Dream* album over and over and over as we began to make our way west and belted out the lyrics: "We can dance until we die / You and I will be young forever." We ate more McDonald's food than I'd ever eaten in my entire life, and since many of the roads we took were cross-country routes for tractor-trailer trucks, we invented games to play with the drivers. Our favorite was pretending that Brittany's Pillow Pet, a unicorn named Penelope, was a horny animal with boobs. We'd scrunch up her chest and shove her out the window, like she was a dirty college girl flashing someone. It was just Brit and me at it again, the wind in our hair as we laughed and laughed and laughed.

We kept up a steady schedule of driving twelve hours a day. We made it a rule to stay only at Holiday Inn Express hotels, since they were super cheap but also clean. Well, most of the time. There was a night in Texas when we couldn't find a single one that wasn't booked solid for the night. We eventually found one with an available room in a really seedy area. The door handle fell almost completely off when we walked in. The overhead lights kept flickering, there were nasty stains all over the bathroom walls and towels, and we found hair in the beds. But it was the middle of the night and we'd already exhausted all other possibilities, so we sucked it up. At least the beds weren't full of spiders. (As far as we could tell!)

We made such good time that we ended up in LA two full days early. We had nowhere to go, so Lisa Nova let us crash at her place while we negotiated with our new landlord to see if we could move in a bit ahead of schedule. He was cool with it, so the day before New Year's Eve we arrived in Culver City and waited for the building manager to come by with the keys.

It was raining, just like the first day I'd set foot in Los Angeles. I thought it was a weird coincidence, since it hardly ever rains here, but I considered it good luck since our first visit had turned out to be so amazing.

Once we got inside the apartment, we were speechless. It was almost unfathomable that it was ours and that we could decorate it and paint it however we wanted. We hadn't gotten a really good look at the place when we'd visited during our last trip, and it was even nicer than we remembered, except that we didn't realize just how unfurnished it would be. We knew we'd have to buy beds, a sofa, and a dining table and chairs, but we didn't realize we'd have to supply our own refrigerator as well. We'd have to build everything from scratch, and I couldn't wait.

We spent the first night driving around and exploring our new city. We found a take-out pizza place, headed back to the apartment, and piled a bunch of our clothes on the floor of the living room so we could sit in comfort while we stuffed ourselves. Luke had invited us to a party at his house, but we just wanted to spend time in our new place. At first we were too giddy to sleep, imagining all of the ways we could decorate the place, but soon all of the excitement caught up with us and we conked out, not even noticing the hard floor underneath us.

The next few days were a whirlwind of painting walls and buying furniture. We still didn't understand just how spread out Los Angeles is, so we ended up driving over an hour to buy furniture, when we easily could have picked up stuff fifteen minutes away. We spent the next week and a half painting all the rooms and assembling Ikea furniture. We got a huge, comfortable sectional sofa for the living room. I painted one wall of my room black and added my name in Japanese and drawings of Totoro, a character from one of my favorite anime films. It was starting to feel like home.

Once we were settled in, it was time to get to work on our first WSP project with Maker Studios. We had met with Lisa and some of the other producers, and they asked us what we wanted our first video to be. We decided on a parody of the Britney Spears song "Hold It Against Me," and we wrote a version where we changed all the lyrics so it was about sleazy douchebags using awful pickup lines to try and get laid. We arrived early on the morning of the shoot and were shocked at how huge the crew was. There was another producer to help us out, a cinematographer to do all the camera work, a cast of extras to use as background dancers, and other YouTube personalities to play the unfortunate victims of our cheesy come-ons. For the first time in our lives, *we* were considered the talent.

It was intimidating at first, but I immediately went into professional mode. The way I saw it, if these people thought I knew what I was doing, then I sure as hell better at least *pretend* to know what I was doing. I turned all of my nervousness into confidence. I wanted to prove to them that I was the best lip-syncher in the world; that I could do anything they asked of me without having to do more than one take. We went out into the streets of LA to shoot a bunch of scenes, and I pretended to ignore the people walking by who gawked and craned their necks to see what the film crew was shooting. It felt like the entire city's eyes were on us, and it felt natural. I'd been making these kinds of videos and acting like a fool in public for so long that it was second nature to me, and once I got over the initial butterflies about performing in front of so many people live—instead of it just being me and Brittany—I was in my element.

Once we wrapped for the day, I told the producer how excited I was.

"I can't believe this is how it's going to be from now on!"

She looked at me like I was crazy. "It isn't. We don't have that kind of budget. You guys are still responsible for producing your own content at least once a week. We can only afford to do things at this level about once a month."

That was still incredible, but now that we had something with such a high production quality, going back to our old do-it-yourself style would look really low budget in comparison. We struggled to come up with content to post in between shooting music videos with Maker Studios, so we mostly relied on "Week in Review" and "Ask WinterSpringPro" bits.

Our first six months in LA flew by, and we began to settle into our new lives. Luke and I started to grow especially close, and my favorite thing was to spend hours at his house playing video games. I'd never had a close male friend before, and it felt great to not feel threatened by a guy. I could be myself around him without any fear that he was going to tease me for acting feminine. The only problem was that Brittany didn't particularly enjoy sitting around his house and watching us play video games, and she was the one with the car.

I started spending more and more time at Luke's house, and I guess that's when Brittany and I started to drift apart. Part of me resented the fact that I did most of the work when it came to WSP. I wished that we could share the editing responsibilities, but she wasn't as comfortable with it and I wasn't crazy about her style of editing, so I'd mostly take over. We also had different views on money. She liked to save hers, but I wanted to go out and discover our new city. Los Angeles isn't exactly the cheapest place to live, but the way I saw it, dining out with Luke and all the other new friends I was making was sort of like investing in my future there. The tension between us slowly started to build, but neither of us was very good with confrontation, so the unease festered.

Luke ended up having a really good idea to help us make more money. When Brittany and I first started doing music parodies, we had found a friend on YouTube we would pay to sing the songs for us because neither of us can carry a tune to save our lives. Then we'd lip-synch along to the results. But since Luke was a musician, he had tons of his own recording equipment. He convinced us that we could sing and record our own lyrics, and then he could touch them up in postproduction to make them sound good. That meant we owned the rights so we could sell the songs on iTunes. The first video that we actually sang on was a parody of Katy Perry's "E.T.," and from then on it was always us. The extra revenue wasn't a whole lot, but it helped ease up some of the financial tension between Brittany and me.

Signs That It's Time to Ditch Your Motel Room and Sleep in the Car

1. Soapscum-lathered clumps of hair in the tub drain.

2. Broken locks on the door or windows.

3. Cigarette burns on the bed cover.

4. Stained towels and/or sheets.

5. Bedbugs. ALWAYS check the mattress edges for these critters. They will try and hitch a ride home with you. They look like reddish little beetles, but honestly, if you see _any_ kind of insect on your mattress, just run.

Avoid Conflict Early On

This is something I'm trying to get better at. I hate conflict and try to avoid it at all costs, but I also know that it's important to express your emotions right off the bat rather than have bad feelings and resentment build up. If you're having an issue with a friend, bring it up sooner rather than later. They might not have any clue that anything is wrong, and working out small stuff early on can prevent a big falling out in the future.

Chapter 13

Breaking Out

I'd started my own personal Joey channel back in 2010, but never really posted much on it. There were fewer than twenty videos there between the time I decided to leave school and when we moved to Los Angeles. But once we arrived and I started to spend more time out and about on my own, I began recording adventures—nothing constant, just fun short updates about my life whenever the mood struck.

Sometimes I'd shoot little behind-the-scenes pieces about WSP videos or film a trip to Disneyland that I took with Luke and Meghan (who had also decided to move to LA), but I didn't take the channel too seriously. I was busy making new friends, in particular a girl named Cat, Meghan's roommate, and another girl, named Whitney, whom I met through Luke. We all clicked and formed a close little circle. It felt wonderful to have a solid group of friends I could count on after struggling for so long.

That June I went home to Massachusetts for a visit. It was my first trip back since moving west, and I was shocked by how gray and drab everything looked in comparison to the perpetual sunshine that always lit everything up in Los Angeles. My mom was in a really good place at the time, so there wasn't any drama and we got along great. She even dyed my hair dark for me in the kitchen, and I was itching to get back to LA the whole time I was there to show it off to my friends.

Brittany had flown back to Massachusetts to visit too, but she had arrived a week earlier than me. I had been devouring *The Hunger Games* books at the time and was utterly obsessed. I'd even started ending all of my vlogs by saying, "May the odds be ever in your favor." So after Brittany left, Whitney, Luke, and I decided to shoot a parody video about the series set to Britney Spears's "I Wanna Go." The three of us wrote all the lyrics, recorded them, and then shot the footage ourselves the day before I left. I played Gale, Luke played Peeta, and Whitney played Katniss. The song was all about the two of us vying for her attention, and in the end she picks both of us.

I finished editing it while I was back home in Massachusetts, and once I posted the video, it absolutely exploded. It became WinterSpringPro's biggest video ever. It was a little odd that Brittany hadn't been part of it, but she didn't mind; she still got her cut of the profits. But it got me thinking about how my creative interests were much more in line with those of my new friends. Luke, Whitney, Meghan, and Cat: they all loved anime and video games and dystopian novels as much as I did. Brit liked these things too, but she wasn't as passionate about them as the rest of us.

In October, Luke's girlfriend at the time, a beauty vlogger named Ingrid Nilsen, persuaded me to participate in something called Vlogtober, a sort of call-to-arms for occasional YouTubers to see if they can post a vlog every day for the entire month. I had so much fun doing it that I decided to keep doing it in November. And then December. And before I knew it, daily vlogging became a full-time gig.

Around the same time that I was starting to lose interest in WinterSpringPro and focus on my own channel, Brittany and I were approached about a potential brand deal. I can't say what it was for, but it doesn't matter because it didn't pan out. But about a week later, the same company reached out about another project. The problem was that they wanted only me, not Brittany.

It was for a website called teen.com, and I quickly learned that they had reached out to Meghan and Cat as well. The three of us went in for a meeting and found out that the website's producers were looking for new hosts for teen.com's YouTube channel, which sounded fun. Then they started tossing some paycheck numbers around and we just about flipped. It was more money than any of us had ever seen in our lives, and we were all struggling to get by at the time.

It was too good an opportunity to pass up, but it presented a lot of problems for me as well. First, I felt guilty that they wanted only me, not Brittany and WinterSpringPro. They were interested in my Joey channel, which at that point had around 70,000 subscribers. The other problem was that in order for me to work with them, I'd need to have my solo channel hosted on Alloy, teen.com's parent site, instead of on Maker Studios' site.

I was too young and naive at the time to know that when it comes to business, it's always best to be honest and upfront. But I was too scared that Maker would say no if they knew I was going to another site to make more money, and so I lied: I said that I wanted to use my solo channel to enter a YouTube video contest, but anyone who was affiliated with a host site was automatically disqualified. Since WinterSpringPro was the channel they'd originally signed, they had no problem giving my little Joey channel back to me to host wherever I wanted. I then turned around and gave my channel to Alloy. (It was hardly an issue for Maker Studios in the end. Disney ended up buying it for 500 MILLION DOLLARS!!!)

Teen.com was a lot of fun at first. I'd work two or three times a week doing shows with Cat and Meghan, and on occasion I'd cover movie junkets. A junket is basically an opportunity for the cast of a new movie to do a ton of interviews at once. They usually get booked into a hotel and a slew of journalists get a chance to meet them. They are huge day-long affairs and pretty exhausting for the celebrities, who have to answer the same questions over and over and over again for different media outlets. The trick to getting a good interview is to come up with questions that they probably hadn't been asked yet.

Over the next few months, I ended up interviewing some pretty big names, like Taylor Swift, Zac Efron, and Rachel Mc-Adams. But I almost peed myself when I got the assignment to interview the cast of *The Hunger Games*. The publicity team at Lionsgate arranged for me to see a screening a month before the movie came out in theaters, and I was openly sobbing during Rue's death scene. I couldn't wait to meet Amandla Stenberg, the girl who played her, so it was a total shock when I walked into the interview and she recognized me!

"Hey, you're the guy who did that *Hunger Games* music video parody!" she said.

"Oh my god, we listened to that over and over on the set," said Alexander Ludwig, the guy who played Cato.

"Look, I have it on my iPod!" said Isabelle Fuhrman, the girl who played Clove. She started singing the lyrics.

The idea that these people were listening to something that I had created while they were shooting what was probably my favorite movie ever at the time blew my mind. It made me feel that I had a special connection to the film, as if I had been a part of it. It was an incredible way to start an interview.

My channel was growing so fast that I barely had time to sit and really think about the fact that my life was changing drastically. I was grateful and excited and scared all at once, and those three emotions became a sort of internal engine for me to keep going. It was what gave me the strength to finally make a decision I'd been delaying for a while: it was time to officially end WinterSpringPro.

Brittany and I hadn't made a video together for a few months at that point, and I think we both knew it was over. She was sad when I told her, but she understood. It wasn't like we were ending our friendship, and she wished me well. She knew that all sorts of different doors were opening for me.

As that year went on, I ended up getting to go to the Teen Choice Awards and MTV Movie Awards and interview celebrities on the red carpet. But instead of the interviews getting easier and becoming more natural, I started to develop more and more anxiety each time I had to do one. I started worrying that I would say the wrong thing or, worse, forget what I was supposed to say and just stand there silently. And there were other things going on in my life at the time that I knew needed more attention—great big life-altering things that I was finally coming to terms with.

Tips for Starting a Vlog

1. Get amped up! You've got to have a lot of energy. If you're not excited, why would your viewers be?

2. Define your personality, and keep it consistent. Find your unique voice.

3. Make daily things like going to the grocery store way more thrilling than they actually are. Get really, really psyched about that sale on kale.

4. It's always good to have someone to bounce things off of. Enlist a friend, family member, or a cute pet (hi, Wolf!) for you to interact with.

5. Come up with something that no one else has ever done before that will make you stand out. If you come up with a concept that you think is awesome, do some Googling to make sure it's not already out there.

Fans IN REAL LIFE

A Q&A with some of Joey's Online Friends

Sophie Dee, Age 13
London, England

Tell me something about yourself. I know this is strange, but I am a cat whisperer. When I meow at my cat, he meows back, and he gives me a very noisy greeting when I get home.

What is your biggest challenge right now? Loneliness. I was never very popular and I don't have a massive amount of friends. Even though my family is here for me, sometimes I just feel alone and unwanted. But watching your videos makes me feel like I'm not the only one, that others understand me and are there to help me.

What are your hopes for the future? To have a job I'd enjoy doing, and to find happiness in simple things, like looking at pretty flowers and enjoying the fresh air. If I've learned anything from you, it's to follow my dreams, that I can achieve anything in life as long as I work hard enough, to keep my head up, and that no dream is too crazy.

Bailey Shepard, Age 15

Atlanta, Georgia

What's one thing you've wanted to tell me?
I actually met some of my closest friends on the Internet because of you!

How's life been lately? Lately, I have been struggling with anxiety. I'm trying to stay calm and stay relaxed more often. Watching your videos also helps calm me down.

Hopes and dreams—go! I want to learn to play bass, I want to go to college, and I want to meet Joey Graceffa sometime soon!

Jess Smith, Age 17
London, England

What surprises people about you? How much I love the cold—I'd always choose winter over summer. Similarly, I don't like hot drinks while they are hot, they have to be cold. Bizarre, I know!

How's college? Stressful. The jump from secondary school to college is so big. Keeping up with course-work deadlines is strenuous because there are usually a hundred things I'd rather be doing than working on my papers!

What do you want to do when you graduate? Preferably something with horses, as they have been a fundamental part of my life since I can remember. I also want to have good people around me, because you are only going to be as good as the people around you.

Yan Schnaiter, Age 13
Fishers, Indiana

What's the coolest birthday gift you've ever gotten? I have a real shining star named after me. It was a birthday gift from one of my best Internet friends. So tonight, twinkling over someone's head and lighting up the night sky somewhere, is my star, Yan.

What scares you? Sometimes I can't help but feel that I'm not living my life to the fullest and doing enough cool stuff.

What's your big wish for the future? To meet you! But another wish I have is to travel the world, meet new people, and document it. I want to take high-quality pictures and videos to share online with people who, for whatever reason, can't travel. I want everyone to have the chance to see what it looks like in some of the world's most exotic locations.

Isabella M., Age 16
New York

What's the craziest way you spent a single day? I watched the entire first season of *Friends* in twenty-four hours.

How are you trying to improve yourself? Lately, I've been encouraging myself to be confident. Sometimes, in this society, I feel as if people have to outdo each other to fit in.

Any wisdom you'd like to share with readers? There isn't a direct solution to suddenly becoming confident overnight. You have to love yourself and constantly remind yourself how important you are. Do things in life that you enjoy and simply stick with it.

Maddie Gilbreth, Age 14
Northern Illinois

What's your big passion right now? I am a huge hockey fan. I play hockey as a starter on a boys' team. Although it is sometimes a challenge, I manage to kick their butts!

What are you trying to overcome? The biggest challenge that I am dealing with is conquering my severe anxiety. Last year, it got so bad that I couldn't even go to school. I could barely leave the house. You have actually played a big role in helping me get through these struggles. As I began to watch you more and more, I discovered that you also deal with anxiety. You are still helping me to this day by showing me it's good to go outside of my comfort zone and to be adventurous.

What do you want to accomplish? My goal is to get my own YouTube channel going and to be successful at it. I don't want to do it for views, popularity, or money. I want to do it so that I can have fun and simply make people happy with any little thing that I can possibly do. All my thanks go out to you for making awesome videos, because without them, I don't know where I'd be.

Michaela Suorsa, Age 14
Frazier Park, California

What makes you unique? I am an identical twin and we were adopted at birth.

How has YouTube changed your life? When I went to VidCon in 2014, I met two amazing people while waiting in line to meet you. We connected because we both had a love for you, and we still keep in touch today!

Tell me something about your family. My mom's babymaker doesn't work, so my whole family is adopted: my twin sister, my brother, and me. We have waited over ten years to get another child and my mom announced to us that we were getting a new little sister, who was nine years old!! I was so excited but also very nervous—I've never had a younger sibling before. But my new little sister, she's awesome! She fits in perfectly. Also, every now and then, she watches Joey's gaming videos with me. She loves them. True bonding! I'm turning her into quite the psychopath!

What is something you've always believed? Everything happens for a reason. Just because things aren't good right now doesn't mean it's always going to be that way, I promise.

Charlotte Killen, Age 16
Northern Ireland, UK

Have we met? I recognize you! We Skyped before, back in September 2014 when I was part of your "Surprising My Subscribers" video! That was the best day of my life, and I got to show you the book I made for you!

What sucks right now? School. It's a struggle! Constant homework, tests, and studying! Luckily, I always have you at the other side of the screen to comfort me when I am finding it tough. It sounds strange I know, but it's true! If I want to relax from homework or need a little break, I will go straight to your channel, and there is my ray of sunshine!

What do you want most in this world? Mainly, to be happy. To enjoy life and try not to be TOO serious. I want to do well in school and try to be successful in everything I do. I would also love to meet you in person someday soon!

Best and Worst
Celebrity Interviews

The coolest famous person I ever got to interview was Taylor Swift. There is nothing weird or manufactured about her—what you see is what you get. She was kind and sweet and immediately started up an actual conversation with me, as opposed to the normal Q&A format that celebrity interviews usually take. She made me feel comfortable, and not once did I think she was putting on an act for me.

The worst experience I ever had with a celebrity was with ... well, I'm not going to tell you her name. I don't want to trash-talk anyone. But I will say that she was a Disney star and that she spent almost the entire interview typing away on her phone and avoiding eye contact. I eventually asked her a totally innocent question about what it feels like to be famous, and she snapped at me and got all huffy, telling me that she wasn't any different now than she had been before becoming a public figure. So I guess that means she's <u>always</u> been a brat!

Ten Celebs I'd Love to Be Best Friends With

Lana Del Rey: We could go on a wine-tasting trip together and then have a picnic in a meadow.

Ellen DeGeneres: I think she'd be a blast to go to Disneyland with.

Miley Cyrus: Hey, girl, let's party!

Marina Diamandis from Marina and the Diamonds: She's Welsh, and I want her to show me all over Europe.

Jennifer Lawrence: All I want to do is hang at her house with her inner circle of friends and talk and laugh.

Nina Debrov: I'd like her to take me shopping. She's got great style.

Nicholas Hoult: I can see us playing games at an arcade together and bonding.

Nicole Kidman: I know she's Australian, but I'd still love to have English high tea with her because she's so classy.

Brendon Urie: Dude, you should totally come over to my house and play video games some time.

Taylor Swift: I feel that we could go to a flea market together and she'd immediately be able to pick out all the coolest stuff from piles of junk.

My Favorite Anime Shows and Movies

These all have very involved plots but I'll do my best to try and describe them simply. But you HAVE to watch these. The layers of depth in each one are utterly mind-blowing. Japanese storytelling is much more interesting and weird and dark than anything I've seen produced in America. They get fantasy right.

Claymore. Forget Panem's thirteen districts. The world in this series has <u>forty-seven</u>, and each one has its own kick-ass female warrior who protects the population from nasty shape-shifters that eat people.

Fullmetal Alchemist. Two brothers lose their mom and then hunt down an alchemist to try and bring her back to life. But that fails, and they end up losing parts of their own body and have to try and find a cure. This description does no justice to how much else happens. Just watch it.

Code Geass. This series takes place in a universe where our world is divided among three super-powers, including one called Britannia. Britannia takes over Japan using giant robots, but a Britannian prince ends up getting stuck in Japan during the destruction and vows to take revenge on his homeland.

My Neighbor Totoro. Hayao Miyazaki is one of the best anime directors ever. In this film, two girls move with their dad to a new house close to the hospital where their mom is staying. They discover a whole world of magical creatures living in and around their new home and have a bunch of adventures with them.

Spirited Away. Another Miyazaki film. In this one, a little girl gets sucked into a spirit world where her parents are turned into pigs and she is forced to work in a witch's bathhouse to try and figure out a way to free herself and them. It won an Academy Award.

Inuyasha. A girl goes to a well and gets sucked inside by a gross centipede demon and ends up five hundred years in the past where she finds out she's a reincarnated priestess. And <u>then</u> shit gets weird.

Chapter 14

Surprise!

I'm gay.

Chapter 15

Dating and Rejection

This is my first time coming out in public, and I'm proud and relieved to be finally telling you all. Ever since I first appeared on YouTube, my sexuality has been the biggest question anyone ever had about me. It was frustrating, especially when I was younger, because while I knew on some level that I had crushes on guys as well as girls, I was nowhere near ready to fully admit it to myself or my friends. Plus, I wanted people to focus on the things I was creating, not whether I wanted to kiss boys.

I think another big reason it took me so long to come out to my friends—and now you—is that I was teased about being feminine so much when I was a kid. Part of me felt that confessing that I was gay would be validating all of the jerks who ever bullied me. Being called gay as an insult had left me emotionally scarred. And although I knew I would probably never speak to any of those kids again in my life, I still felt that I had to stand my ground against them. When it came right down to it, I just didn't want to be gay. And part of me was frustrated that just because I acted feminine, everyone automatically assumed I was gay. Sure, it was true, but I didn't want to feed into a stereotype just because I was acting in a way that came naturally to me.

So I continued to avoid and ignore the question. My life is so public as it is, and I needed something of my own that I

157

could keep for myself, especially after I moved out to Los Angeles and first got the guts up to start exploring my sexuality.

It's strange to live with knowledge about yourself that you believe is never going to become part of your actual physical life. For a long time, I genuinely believed that I would always like girls and keep my boy crushes in this tiny little place in the back of my head. But pretty much as soon as I moved to Los Angeles and faced a whole world of dating possibilities, I finally had to own up to the fact that there is a HUGE difference between thinking a girl is pretty and being sexually attracted to her.

Before I could come out to my friends, though, I had to come out to myself. Since I was already aware of those feelings in me, it wasn't some big flash of light, but a very gradual process of getting comfortable with the fact that these hidden thoughts were becoming dominant. (And truthfully, all the manly LA eye candy probably helped speed things along.)

In addition to wanting to keep part of my life private, another big reason that it took me so long to publicly come out is that I know there are people who look to me as a role model. I take that responsibility seriously, and I didn't want to announce something that I was still figuring out for myself. If there were closeted kids watching my videos and they needed a positive figure to look to, I wasn't the right person for a long time. I still had a lot of learning and growing to do on my own before I could offer any kind of advice to someone else.

I'm now in a place in my life where I'm proud to be who I am, and I'm tired of hiding and being afraid to share certain experiences. I want to be a person others can look up to and help teach others that liking the same sex is a normal thing. That's just how you were created, and there is no shame in that. I don't ever want anyone to have to feel afraid or feel the need to pretend to be someone they're not. I know firsthand how excruciating that can be, and it's important to remember that while we live in a time where it's easy to say things like, "Being gay is no big deal," a lot of people still aren't yet comfortable with who they are. It's a delicate place to be, and my advice to anyone struggling with that mind-set is to take things at your own pace. It's *your* life, and you shouldn't feel any pressure to admit feelings to people when you still haven't fully processed them for yourself.

If your feelings for the same sex are getting stronger, try asking yourself what it would take for you to be ready to tell other people. Are you waiting to fall into a relationship first, or do you just want to gain a little experience? That's fine, but I think some people get too caught up in that waiting game. They feel that they already need to have someone in their life before coming out to family and friends, as if having a companion validates the fact to others. It doesn't. Remember that the only person you should be trying to make happy while coming out is yourself.

For all you straight people out there, if you have a guy friend who acts overly feminine or a girlfriend who is super butch, don't ask them if they're gay. They might not be, or they might not be ready to admit it. The best thing to do is what my mom and Nicole did so many years ago in our kitchen. They gently and subtly assured me that if I ever realized I was gay, they would be there to support me no matter what. You can't force anyone out of the closet. It's a deeply personal decision, and the best thing we can continue to do as a society is keep working at making this world a place where there's no need to feel shame about who you are, which is why I'm finally choosing to talk about my early experiences with guys.

Well, *early* is probably the wrong word. I got a bit of a late start when it came to dating. Actually, a very late start. I didn't even have my first kiss until I was twenty-one years old.

That's right, *twenty-one*. By that age, most other kids have lost their virginity, had a nude selfie go viral in their school, or been arrested for having sex in public. Not me. But by the time I'd been in Los Angles for almost a year, my feelings about guys were so strong that I couldn't ignore them anymore. They came to a head at Whitney's twenty-first birthday party.

We celebrated at a Mexican restaurant in Santa Monica, and she had invited a bunch of her friends I'd never met before. When I arrived, they were all crowded around her at one end of the table, and I ended up sitting at the other end with Luke and Brittany. But a guy sitting close to Whitney immediately caught my eye. He had a swimmer's build, with swept-back dark hair and devilish eyes that crinkled when he grinned. I was wishing that I had gotten to sit closer to them when I heard the waitress ask if I wanted anything to drink.

"A peach margarita," I said, without hesitation. "No salt." I wasn't twenty-one quite yet then, but since we were all obviously there celebrating Whitney's twenty-first and everyone else was drinking, I hoped I could get away with it. And I did!

As dinner wound down, everyone started to make plans to take Whitney to a bar, which bummed me out. Our waitress might have turned a blind eye to my drink order, but there was no way I was getting past a bouncer without an ID.

"Let's pregame at my place first," Luke offered. "That way Joey can hang out with us for a while longer."

Everyone thought this was a great idea, and as soon as we got to Luke's house, he whipped out a huge bottle of Captain Morgan rum.

"Okay, we're gonna play a game," Luke said. "Everyone

stand in a circle. When the bottle comes to you, take a big chug and pass it to the person to your right, but you have to say 'cannonball coming' before it leaves your hand; otherwise you have to drink again."

It hardly seemed to qualify as a drinking game. It's not like anyone forgot to say the words—unless they specifically wanted to take an extra swig. But it did the trick, and before long we were all pretty loopy. I got introduced to the guy I'd been checking out at the dinner table. His name was Kyle, and as the game went on, we kept meeting each other's eyes. At that point, I'd already discovered that he was gay because he'd mentioned that he thought some male movie star was cute.

Every time we looked at each other, I'd turn away fast, only to slowly move my eyes back and find he was still staring. I was confused and excited. It was the first time I'd ever been attracted to a guy who seemed to be into me as well. But the feelings were all too new and I didn't know what to do with them. I couldn't imagine the attraction leading to anything, but at the same time, part of me wanted it to. I wished I could talk to a friend about what I was going through, but I couldn't bring myself to do that. It was just too scary and big and new.

About fifteen people were at the party, and it turned out that a lot of the guys were gay. Hanging out with them was totally different from hanging out with straights. Suddenly I could be my own silly self and not have to worry about any-one being a jerk by making some snide remark about my act-ing feminine or goofy. I pretended to be a pirate and chased Brittany around the house with a foam sword while everyone cheered us on. A little while later, I found myself gnawing on a pumpkin spice–scented candle to see if it tasted the way it smelled. (Big surprise, it didn't.) I also knew in that moment it was time to sober up. Attempting to eat a candle is hardly the mark of someone who is in control.

I flopped down on the couch and pointed to one of the guys. "Get me some water!" I shouted in a faux British accent, as if they were all my personal butlers. I was half-kidding, but he actually did, and so I spent the next half hour ordering different gay guys to fetch me water while pretending they were my servant boys. They ate it up.

After I got tired of ordering them around, I went into the kitchen to refill my water glass. The hard fluorescent lighting hurt my eyes after sitting in the dim living room for so long, and Kyle was squatting next to the fridge, fishing around for a beer. He stood up when I entered. "Watthh up," he mumbled. "Wanna beer?"

"No thanks," I said and leaned against the counter next to Luke's blackened stovetop. "I'm just getting some water."

Kyle crossed the kitchen and leaned strangely close to me, enough to make me a little nervous. "So how do you know Whitney?" I asked.

He launched into some sort of convoluted list of names and events that I couldn't quite follow, but I nodded along, pretending to understand what the hell he was talking about. But I couldn't pay attention at all because I was so distracted by how cute he was.

He finally stopped talking and there was a bit of awkward silence when suddenly he closed his eyes and lurched toward me. Everything went into slow motion, and I was terrified as his lips crept closer and closer to my face. I looked down and stepped away at the last second, so he stumbled forward. "I . . . um, I have to check my phone," I said as I fled from the kitchen into the living room.

I sat back down on the couch next to Luke and Brittany and watched as Kyle left the kitchen, crawled along the wall to the bathroom, and slammed the door shut. We all heard him start puking, and his friends ran to the door and started pounding on it until he let them in.

I didn't leave Luke's and Brittany's sides for the rest of the party. I tried to concentrate on what people were saying, but all I could think was, *Did Kyle really just try and kiss me?* Had I imagined it? Maybe he was just so drunk that he was swaying and he leaned in too close. But no—I may not have ever been kissed before, but I've seen enough movies to know what it looks like when someone goes for it. Plus, the more I thought about it, there had been a sort of energy in the air between us— something I'd never felt before, like a chemical reaction was sending out invisible rays signaling that this guy was into me. I started regretting not letting it happen.

Luke and I and a few other people at the party ended up playing *Mario Kart* for a couple more hours while I sobered up so I could drive home. I watched Kyle slink out of the bathroom and leave with his friends, but he didn't turn around to say good-bye to anyone.

That night, I couldn't sleep. I kept wondering what would have happened if I had just let him kiss me. *I did the right thing*, I told myself. He may have been cute, but I didn't want my first kiss ever to be with a guy who was completely trashed. Still, I was sort of mad at myself for chickening out. I volleyed those two conflicting thoughts around in my head until I finally fell asleep around dawn.

I called Whitney in the morning and told her what happened.

"No way," she said. "I'm so sorry. He must have been really drunk. Kyle can get a little out of control."

"It's okay. It was funny, I guess," I said.

She was silent for a minute, and I felt I could read her mind through the phone. She was wondering if it was something that maybe I *wanted* to happen.

Luke was more direct when I told him what had happened later that day. "So, if he did kiss you, would you have liked that?" he asked.

"No, definitely not," I said automatically. He gave me a look, like *Really?* "I mean, I don't know. I don't know about these things. I don't know what I like."

"It's totally okay if you did want it," he said. "Or if you ever decide you do. No one is going to judge you. I hope you know that."

"I know," I mumbled and changed the subject.

Over the next few days, I kept replaying the moment in the kitchen in my head and imagining different scenarios. In one, Kyle started groping me and I slapped him. In another, we had a really gentle, romantic kiss. In yet another, someone walked in on us just as we started to kiss, and I saw myself dying of embarrassment and shame.

But the more I thought about it, the less shame I felt. Everyone around me was so accepting, it seemed crazy that I couldn't be as kind to myself.

Luke had another party at his house about a week later, and Kyle showed up. He walked right up and cornered me in a passageway between the kitchen and dining room. I caught a whiff of a sexy sandalwood cologne, and my palms immediately started to sweat.

"Whitney told me that I tried to kiss you last week," he said.

I saw her standing in the corner over his shoulder and shot her dagger eyes. She shrugged and smiled and turned to talk to someone else.

"Huh?" I said, playing dumb. "Oh, wait, that? Brittany told me that she thought she saw you trying to kiss me and I didn't remember it, so I think I mentioned it to Whitney or something. I never actually told anyone you tried to kiss me." I tried to laugh like it was no big deal, but the only sound that came out of my mouth was an awkward, high-pitched squeak. I wanted to disappear.

"I probably did try, and I'm so sorry," he said. "I was smashed, I don't remember anything about that night. I was sick all the next day, and apparently here too."

Great. Kyle trying to kiss me was probably one of the defining moments of my life, and he didn't even remember it.

"It's fine. Whatever," I said and watched him walk back into the crowd.

I looked around the party at the rest of the people there. It was about twice the size of the last one, and there were a lot of gay guys around. I prayed that the situation might repeat itself with someone else, and I kept hanging out in the kitchen, hoping that someone would walk in and find me there all alone. I wasn't about to try and hit on anyone myself, though. I wasn't ready to take the lead, and I think I knew deep inside that even if someone *had* tried to kiss me again at that particular party, I still wouldn't have let it go anywhere. I just wasn't there yet. But thanks to Kyle's drunk, stumbling efforts, my closet door was starting to open.

•   •   •

A few weeks later, Luke spent a long, grueling day shooting a video for a song that a friend of his had written. He and the rest of the musicians had worked their butts off, and afterward he invited me out to dinner with the other performers and some of the members of the crew.

Luke was busy talking with everyone from the shoot, so I got stuck at the other end of the table, mixed in with a bunch of people I didn't know. It was a pretty big group that included friends of people who were at the shoot, and I felt that Luke was ignoring me, so I sulked a little, but a guy sitting directly across from where I ended up started chatting with me. Sam had short brown hair and was wearing a soft-looking, faded red-and-black-checked flannel shirt. I couldn't tell if he was gay, but he seemed really interested in talking to me; he kept asking me all these questions about YouTube and my videos. At the end of the night he asked for my number.

"We should go grab lunch and talk some more," he said. It didn't seem that he was asking me out on a date, though. He was so casual about it, and I figured he just wanted to discuss more YouTube stuff. I mean, I *thought* maybe he was gay because of certain little things, like the way he leaned in close while talking to me, but I didn't want to assume anything. He told me to meet him the next day at a place called Tender Greens in West Hollywood.

Now, I'd never been to West Hollywood before. For those of you not from Los Angeles, it's one of the gayest neighborhoods in the country, right up there with the Castro District in San Francisco. Except that in WeHo, the sidewalks are crawling with cute, toned boys with perfect hair instead of leather daddies. But I was so clueless that none of the area's personality registered when I first met up with Sam for lunch. To be fair, I was distracted—I'd just found out that I'd booked a modeling gig with a photographer. It was going to be a pretty elaborate shoot, set up like a big joyous birthday party, except that I was going to be really sad and depressed in the photos. I was excited about it, and I told Sam all about it as soon as we sat down, including the photographer's name.

"Oh really?" he laughed. "I used to fool around with him."

So he *was* gay. But what the heck did "fooling around" mean exactly? I sort of knew it meant at least kissing, but I reasoned that it could also mean that they were playing video games, tag, or hide-and-go-seek together. God, I was *such* a prude! I felt utterly clueless.

He was wearing another flannel shirt, blue and gray this time, and not that what a person wears should necessarily signify anything, but his look still somehow radiated "straight dude." Even though I was happy for the confirmation that he liked guys, hearing him talk about fooling around with someone else gave me a tiny ping of jealousy.

"Small world," I said.

I changed the subject quickly, and the lunch flew by. He was easy to talk to and seemed genuinely interested in the work I was doing. He was an assistant to an indie film producer so I asked him a lot about that. After we finished up, I figured we were done, but as soon as we got out to the sidewalk, he asked if I wanted to grab some frozen yogurt for dessert.

"Sure," I said, and we walked a block to a seemingly innocent place called Yogurt Stop. But when we got inside, I immediately started blushing. All of the flavors were named after some sort of ridiculous gay innuendo. I scanned the list of options like "I'm Comin' Out Cake Batter," "Let Me French Kiss Your Vanilla," and "Hallelujah, It's Raining Red Velvet Men." (I suddenly heard an echo from the past in the back of my head: *"It's raining Joey's guts, amen!"*)

Most of the names were laughable and didn't even make sense—I mean, what the hell is a "red velvet man"? But they still made me uncomfortable. I selected the most innocent one I could find: "Love Lipstick Latte." Sam got "Ride It Real Good Raspberry," and I felt my cheeks turn bright red.

We grabbed a table outside, and that's when I started noticing that the sidewalk was dominated by men, many of them wearing tight clothes, most of them holding hands or walking dogs small enough to fit into an evening clutch.

"Where are we?" I whispered.

"What do you mean?" he asked. "West Hollywood."

"Why does everyone look so . . . gay?"

He was cracking up. "Have you seriously never been here before?"

"No," I said, my jaw dropping at the sight of a sculpted jogger who was obviously not wearing any underwear.

"Where have you been hiding?" Sam teased.

"I mean, I work all the time," I said. Which was true, but I think I was actually a little too scared to do a lot of city exploring on my own, especially to places like this. "Also, I don't really have any gay or bi friends," I added.

"Well, we should fix that," he said, staring at me as he licked his spoon. "Hey, you should really come to the Electric Guest concert with me next Wednesday. I bet you'd really like them. A whole bunch of my friends are coming too."

I could barely handle being alone with him. I couldn't imagine how scary it would be to hang out with him surrounded by a bunch of strangers. So I lied and told him I had plans.

He looked disappointed, but said we should try and hang out again soon.

We started texting a lot over the next week. Both of us were busy with work, but when we discovered we both had an upcoming afternoon free, he said we should go see a movie.

That sounds fun, I wrote. Although what I wanted to write was, "I need to know if this is a date or not!"

His response: *Cool, it's a date! I mean, it's a plan. Not a date.*

That didn't help things at all. I had no idea how to reply to that so I just asked what theater I should meet him at. When I arrived, he was wearing yet another flannel shirt, this one with green and black checks. This guy *really* loved flannel. He had already paid for the tickets—we were seeing a CIA thriller, *Safe House*—and we ran inside just as the trailers started. As we sat down, his leg brushed up against mine, but I didn't move away, and neither did he. I couldn't concentrate on the movie at all. Instead, I wondered if we were going to hold hands. I kept sneaking glances at him out of the corner of my eye. His profile was lit up by all the action on the screen, but he didn't look back at me. A darkened movie theater seemed like it might be a cool place for a first kiss, but I decided I didn't want the experience to happen over a soundtrack of Denzel Washington getting waterboarded. Still, our legs remained touching throughout the whole movie.

He had to leave right after to get back to work, and we hugged good-bye. I still felt that he was keeping me in the friend zone, but when he asked me the next day to go out to dinner and a movie with him, I knew it was official. I may have been inexperienced, but I knew that you don't ask someone you just met to dinner and a movie without it being an actual date. It would be my first real date, ever.

It was rocky from the start.

Where do you want to get dinner? he texted. *Do you like exotic food?*

I don't. AT ALL. *How exotic are we talking?* I asked.

There's this place called Animal. Google it.

169

I'd heard of the restaurant before—it had been getting a lot of press—but when I checked the website, I saw that the menu was full of stuff like chicken liver toast, veal brains with apricot puree, and crispy pig head with bulldog sauce. I was pretty sure that the last ingredient didn't include any actual bulldog, but based on all the other weird crap they were offering, I didn't want to take any chances.

Oh god, I wrote. *That might be a little too extreme for me. I just tried oysters for the first time last week.*

Ha, okay. Any other places on your mind?

Sorry I'm so lame.

You suck. I'm done. Have a nice life. Enjoy McDonald's.

I knew he was just joking, but it still hurt my feelings a little. *Fine*, I wrote. *I will. I love McDonald's.*

Haha, ok. You pick the place.

I suggested Rock Sugar, a pan-Asian spot in Studio City at the Westfield Mall. Some friends had recently recommended it, and he agreed.

That's when the reality of it all suddenly sunk in: I was going on my very first date, and it was going to be with a guy. There was no going back—I was officially acting on the one thing I didn't think I'd ever be able to do. And it was something I couldn't keep to myself anymore. I needed someone to talk to about it, someone who could support me.

I ended up blurting it out to Cat.

We hadn't seen each other in a while, so we made plans to see a movie, and afterward we went to dinner at a little outdoor café near the theater. Once we had ordered our food, she settled back in her chair and looked at me.

"So, how's your love life? Anyone you're interested in?"

Is it that obvious? I must have been grinning like a lovesick puppy.

"Tell me!" she said, leaning forward.

"It's kind of complicated," I said, trying to avoid eye contact and fiddling with my fork. There was a long silence and I couldn't make the words come out of my mouth. Lucky for me, she broke the ice.

"Are you gay?" she blurted out.

For the first time in my life, I wasn't offended by the question. "No, I'm bi . . . I think," I said. I felt a flood of relief at finally saying it out loud, even though I wasn't ready to say that I was full-on gay. *Bisexual* felt safer because it suggested that I was leaving all options for my future open. *Baby steps*, I thought.

"Oh my god, that's awesome!" she squealed. She was practically jumping up and down in her seat. "So you like someone?"

"I've been talking to this guy named Sam that I met through Luke. We have a date. My first. Ever."

She squealed some more and demanded to see photos of him on my phone.

"He's cute," she said, thumbing through his Facebook profile. "It's gonna be great."

The next day, I knew it was time to tell Nicole. Now that I'd finally said the words out loud, I needed the kind of reassurance I knew I could only get from someone who's known and loved me my entire life. Her reaction was pretty much the same as Cat's. She was so happy that she almost started crying with joy. I was so relieved.

"Do you realize that this is probably one of the first times you've ever been truly open with me about your feelings?" she asked. "You've always shied away from expressing what's really going on in your head. This is such a huge and important step, and I'm so proud of you. I want to hear all about the date afterward!"

Whitney was next, and she was nothing but supportive too, except for one thing: "I can't believe you told Cat before me," she pouted.

Luke was thrilled for me too. But despite the universal support I was getting, I started having some doubts. I can't emphasize enough that this was my FIRST DATE EVER, and I had no idea how I was supposed to act while I was on it. I genuinely didn't know if it would be different from hanging out with a friend. So I did what I always do when I need to know something: I turned to YouTube. Searches for "How to act on a first date" led me to a channel run by two women called The Wing Girls, who offered up all sorts of advice about having your first kiss, like practicing beforehand with your own hand, or the inside of your arm, or on a cantaloupe. I wasn't about to make out with a melon, so I clicked on another video, "What to Talk About on Your First Date." Basically it said not to reveal too much, don't go too deep. I could do that.

Whitney sent me a text on the afternoon of the date. *What are you going to wear?* I was too busy to write back because I still had no idea. I had laid out four outfits on my bed to choose from before I showered, so I'd have time to really think about each one while I got cleaned up. I spent a good twenty minutes on my hair, getting my long emo bangs to swoop perfectly across my forehead to the right. I surveyed my clothing options and eventually decided to go casual—a pair of dark blue skinny jeans and a tee-shirt.

I left the apartment really early in case of traffic, but the roads were fine, and I found myself with thirty minutes to kill after I arrived. Since the restaurant was located in a mall, I figured that shopping might help calm me down a little, so I wandered into a nearby Sperry store and quickly got lost in shoe land. I tried on several pairs before narrowing my selections down to two options. One was sea green, the other royal blue. I was staring at the ground, studying them intently when I heard a voice behind me.

"Go with the green."

I turned around and Sam was standing there smiling, dressed in a gray-and-white-striped dress shirt. I silently rejoiced. *He didn't wear flannel!* If there had been any lingering doubt as to whether this was a real date, the absence of his usual bro uniform erased it. He reached out and gave me a hug, and my heart felt like it was about to explode out of my chest.

"The green? You think?" I asked as we separated.

"Definitely. The other ones are too bright."

I paid for the shoes and we headed to the restaurant. We ordered some food and he ordered sake. "Never order it hot," he told me with a conspiratorial whisper. "It means it's a crap brand of sake if they serve it that way. Get it cold."

I nodded distractedly as I racked my brain for something light and not too deep to talk about. "Oh, I've got that birthday party shoot with your friend tomorrow!" I said.

"Yeah, I know. I was just texting with him right before I got here," he said.

A panicky thought entered my mind. *What if they're still fooling around?* The prospect made me feel queasy, but it also reminded me that I still didn't have the address of where I was supposed to show up the next day. I shot the guy a quick e-mail from my phone under the table and turned my attention back to Sam. I desperately tried to come up with something funny and charming to say, but before I got a chance, he suddenly, out of nowhere, goes: "I can be a pretty controlling person sometimes."

I was no expert, but even I knew this was a terrible conversation starter for a first date. But maybe he was just trying to be real and upfront with me. Maybe I was being too old school in my thinking.

"Really?" I said, not sure how to respond. "Why do you think that is?"

He didn't go into specifics. "I don't like to talk about it," he said, "but I feel like I'm kind of messed up right now. Sometimes I can't get out of bed. I never leave the house and just play video games."

"I like *Mario Kart*," I offered, trying to lighten the mood. "I'm really good at it!"

"Video games are actually dangerous for me, though," he said. "I just spend the entire day staring at the screen, avoiding work."

What is wrong with this guy? I thought. *Is he trying to murder our date?*

I gave it another shot, trying once more to change the subject. "I saw a preview screening of *The Hunger Games* a few weeks ago for my teen.com job," I said. "It's really good."

"I also have OCD. That might be why I always want to control things."

I had no idea where to go from there, so I just kept talking about *The Hunger Games*. The date was turning into an absolute disaster. I was confused. Why was he saying so many negative things about himself? Was he trying to give me some sort of warning, that this was destined to go nowhere?

The waitress saved me when she took our order, providing

enough of a distraction to get him on track talking about normal stuff. "I hear *John Carter* is awful," I said, referring to the movie we were going to see later. "But I still want to give it a chance. I'm kind of a sci-fi and fantasy nerd. I actually got in trouble for posting a personal video about *The Hunger Games* screening I went to. All the reviews were supposed to be embargoed."

"Ooh, a rebel," he laughed, and I relaxed. The conversation stayed pretty light and fun for the rest of dinner. But as I was confirming the movie time on my phone, disaster struck in the form of the check.

The waitress slid a fake leather billfold containing the slip of paper onto the table and said, "Whenever you're ready." It sat there between the two of us, but I refused to break eye contact with Sam. I nodded and laughed at whatever it was he was saying, but internally I was freaking out.

I had no idea which one of us was supposed to pay.

The Wing Girls hadn't covered this at all. I guess I'm old-fashioned because I always assumed that the guy picks up the check. But we were two guys! If I had been taking a girl out on a date, I would have reached for it immediately. And maybe I was just being too heteronormative, but since he had asked me out and he was older, wasn't he supposed to pay? Plus, well, he was more experienced than I was. It seemed like the gallant thing for him to do. But he hadn't made a single move to reach for it, and even though he was in the middle of a story I couldn't concentrate on a thing he said. That little billfold was taunting me. *This is absurd*, I told myself, and just as I resolved to pick it up and pay, he slid his credit card out and handed it, along with the check, to the passing server.

I was so flustered that I don't even remember if I said thank you. I think I did. I *hope* I did.

I decided to make up for it by paying for the movie tickets. As soon as we got to the theater across the mall, I started to walk faster. "Don't worry, I got these!" I said.

"Wait, hang on a second," he called out just as I reached the ticket counter. "My boss is calling me." He waved me over, so I walked slowly back.

He had his back to me but it sounded like he was arguing about something. "Can't it wait until tomorrow?"

I looked at my phone. It was almost 10:00 p.m.

Sam shoved his phone in his pocket and turned back to me. "Aw, man, I'm sorry. I gotta go."

"What happened?"

"My boss is making me go home and work on some stuff." He looked off into the distance.

"Can't you use your phone to do it?" I hinted.

"No, I need my computer." He met my eyes for a second before quickly looking away again, like he felt guilty.

I waited for a few seconds before saying anything to see if he was going to invite me along to hang out while he did whatever he needed to do. Was I being ditched? *Oh no*, I thought. *Was he faking that phone call? What if it's because I didn't pay for dinner? But I was about to make up for it! I would have gotten popcorn too!*

"That sucks," I finally said when he didn't say anything more. "He really won't let you do it tomorrow?"

"No, I gotta go. Hey, where did you park?"

"The garage, ground level," I mumbled.

"I'm up on the fifth. Can you give me a ride to my car?"

"Sure," I said, and gave him a big fake smile. I had to pretend that I didn't mind he was leaving, but I was bummed out. I genuinely had no idea if I was getting dumped or if he was being legit with me, but I couldn't just come right out and ask. If I did and it turned out this was some sort of real work emergency, I'd look like a whiney weirdo. I had to take the high road and act like this was no big deal, when inside I was dying. Aside from all his early talk about what a mess he was and then my stress about the check, I actually thought the date was going relatively well.

We got to my car, and I drove him to his in silence.

"Right there," he said, pointing to a red Mini Cooper as we rounded a corner.

"Okay, well, bye," I said.

I turned to look at him and he started to lean in. *Oh hell no*, I thought. *I am not wasting my first kiss on some guy who's skipping out on our first date.* I turned my head far from his face and gave him a hug instead, but at least it was a close one so that our cheeks brushed together.

"Hope everything is okay with work," I said.

"It'll be fine. Enjoy your new shoes!" he said as he slammed the door behind him.

The shoes. *Damn it.* After all that, I'd left them in the restaurant. All I wanted to do was go home and wallow in my disappointment, but I had to go back and collect them.

Sam texted me a photograph of the outside of the restaurant the next day, with a message that said, *I liked it so much, I'm already back! J/K, just driving past.*

I didn't hear from him again for three months. I also never heard anything back from his photographer friend about our photo shoot that day. I had cleared my whole schedule for it, but the guy Sam used to fool around with never replied about where I was supposed to go. I sent two more e-mails the day it was supposed to happen and finally gave up around noon.

I grew paranoid that Sam had talked crap about me. *Yeah, I could practically hear him saying. And he didn't even offer to split the check! Let alone pay for the whole thing.*

Not only had I been ditched during my first date ever, it looked like maybe I had lost a job over it too. I didn't want to let it get me down—I was really proud of myself for even getting the courage up to go out with a guy—but the double blow made me question whether dating was even worth the time. Maybe I'd be better off alone.

Cool Websites Dedicated to the LGBTQ Experience

Hrc.org. The Human Rights Campaign is the biggest civil rights organization devoted to equality for gay, lesbian, bisexual, and transgender people. Its website lists the campaigns it is currently working on in your state and tells you what you can do to get involved.

Splcenter.org. The cool thing about the Southern Poverty Law Center is that it doesn't just fight against bigotry against the LGBTQ community.

It works for any group that's discriminated against. The center has a staff of lawyers with the power to help change laws and maintains a huge database of hate groups to watch out for.

Thetrevorproject.org. If you ever have feelings about harming yourself, go to this website immediately. It has an awesome crisis intervention and suicide prevention hotline for LGBTQ youth and lots of educational resources for grown-ups and kids.

Itgetsbetter.org. Visibility is an important part of the LGBTQ movement. Seeing people tell stories about themselves that mirror your own experiences can make a colossal difference when you're struggling with self-doubt about your sexuality.

Lambdalegal.org. If you are being discriminated against because of your sexuality or gender identity, reach out to Lambda Legal. Its help desk can provide all sorts of legal advice so that you know your rights.

Dating 101: How to Deal with a Lull in the Conversation

1. Acknowledge the awkwardness: Saying something like, "Aren't first dates weird?" will probably relieve the tension for both of you. Then you can unite in making fun of the whole experience.

2. Don't be scared to ask a totally random question, even if it sounds weird—something like: "Where would you live if you could live anywhere in the world?" The answer will probably be revealing.

3. Ask the other person if he or she watches my videos. And if this person is a hater, dump him or her immediately!

4. DON'T text at the table. It's rude on a first date. If you're desperate for quick advice, excuse yourself to the bathroom and text your friend there.

5. Favorite movies are always a safe bet. You might get into a lively debate about whether <u>Mockingjay</u> really should have been split up into two movies.

Chapter 16

Long Distance

Twelve weeks after Sam ditched me, I got a text from him. *Hey random question. Are you going to VidCon?*

That wasn't a random question at all. Of course I was going to VidCon. By that point it had grown to be a huge event for any YouTuber. But more important, why was he writing to me now, out of nowhere? I'd spent the past few months trying to get him out of my head and not even think about dating. Instead, I focused all of my energy and resolve on my videos. I decided to ignore the text, but that lasted all of about forty seconds.

Yes. Are you?

I was going to, but it looks like all the passes are sold out . . .

So that's why he was getting in touch: he wanted to use me to get tickets. I was angry for a minute, but I decided to get over it. I didn't want to let him get to me, and being spiteful would just end up making things worse. Plus, I had to admit to myself that even though I knew he was just taking advantage of my access, I still kind of wanted to see him. All those months of not knowing what I had done wrong had left me confused. I was hoping that if I saw him, I could at least get some kind of closure. So I gave him the e-mail address of a contact I knew could hook him up.

VidCon was overlapping that year with another conference that I desperately wanted to go to—the Anime Expo. I'd recently become friends with a really cool girl named Kalel.

181

We bonded over our love of cosplay, and she got major bonus points in my book for changing her name from Kristin to the same one Superman was originally given on Krypton. We had been planning our costumes for the Anime Expo for weeks. I was going as Nintendo's Kid Icarus, and she was going as Snow White.

I was also going to be spending most of VidCon with two YouTuber friends from England, Jim and Tanya, filming stuff from the conference on their channel with them in addition to attending a bunch of panels and going to parties. I just wanted to enjoy my time at the convention without getting dragged into Sam's life again.

I decided to rent a hotel room with Cat at a Hilton near the convention center in Anaheim so we wouldn't have to keep driving back and forth each day. I arrived a little late on the first night, and after dropping my stuff off in the room, I went to a party hosted by District Lines, a company that makes merchandise like tee-shirts and tote bags for YouTubers. The event happened to be taking place at our hotel, so all I had to do was go downstairs to one of the conference spaces. The room was dark, illuminated only by pink and blue lights that streaked up the walls from the floor. The music was deafening, and everyone was wearing glow necklaces and dancing.

As I stood there letting my eyes adjust to the dark, a familiar-looking guy walked right up to me. It took a second for me to recognize him as Mike, a gay vlogger from Ohio whom I'd met briefly at another YouTube conference not too long ago. He was cute—shorter than me, with blondish brown hair that he wore swooped up off his face.

"Hey, Joey, good to see you!" he shouted over the music.

"You too! Where's the bar in this place?"

"I'll get you a drink. What do you want?"

That's sweet, I thought. "Um, a tequila sunrise." I'd just turned twenty-one and loved the freedom to order whatever I wanted.

"Coming right up."

I chatted with a few YouTube friends I hadn't seen in a long time, but right as Mike came over with my drink, I spotted Jim and Tanya across the room. "Thanks, bye!" I said as I ran off to greet them. Not very nice, I know, but I was starting to think that maybe Mike liked me, and that made me so nervous I didn't know what else to do. I hung out with Jim and Tanya for about an hour before the party ended and we had to leave. I decided to just head to my hotel room and prepare for the next day's craziness, so I said my good-byes and made my way toward the door when Mike suddenly appeared beside me. "Hey, what's your number?" he asked. "We should hang out while I'm in town!"

"Sure," I said. I still couldn't tell for absolute sure if he was hitting on me or if he genuinely just wanted to hang out, but he seemed really nice so I figured it couldn't hurt either way.

It was a good thing I went to bed early. From the moment I stepped into the convention center the next day, it was a nonstop tornado of screams and bright lights and crowds. I met lots of viewers who kept coming up to me wearing tee-shirts with my name on them. One of them gave me a cute Soot Sprite stuffed animal from *Spirited Away.* Another bunch of girls serenaded Whitney, Cat, and me with the lyrics Luke and I had written to our *Hunger Games*/Britney Spears video parody. I got proposed to and given an actual ring by a really sweet girl at a Mega Meet Up panel. I signed hundreds of autographs. It was all so much fun that it made it easy to put the whole Sam mess out of my mind once and for all. I didn't need someone like him in my life when I had so much love and support coming from all these other people.

Oh, who was I fooling? In the back of my head, I was totally hoping that he would text me and want to hang out. I kept thinking it would be so cool to have someone special to share all of this with. But Sam never reached out. I began to wonder again if maybe Mike was a possibility, and I kept an eye out for him the whole time, but I didn't see him until the end of the second day.

I was hanging out with Whitney at our overpriced hotel bar with a bunch of other random vloggers, trying to figure out what to do that evening, when I saw Mike strolling across the lobby with a bottle of vodka tucked under his arm. I nudged Whitney and pointed. "Maybe he'll share with us."

"Hey, Mike!" I shouted and waved. He was with a few friends, and they all came over with him.

"What's up?" I asked.

"We're going to a room party. Come with us!"

I glanced at Whitney and could tell she was feeling the same way I was. We'd spent the whole day surrounded by strangers, and we preferred to be with a smaller group at that point.

"Bummer," I said. "We were just going back to our room. You should stop by before you go and bring that bottle!"

Everyone in his group seemed a little tipsy. They were taking pictures and spinning off into their own little groups, so he shrugged. "Sure. Lead the way!"

Once in the room, we poured drinks and put on some music, danced around, and caught up on our VidCon experiences.

"Someone proposed to me today," I shouted over the music.

"Guy or girl?" he asked.

"Girl."

"Lucky bitch."

Whitney rolled her eyes. "I gotta go. My sister is waiting up for me. Have fun, boys."

As soon as she was gone, I lowered the music and sat on the side of one of the beds. Mike fell back and then suddenly sat up cross-legged on the other.

"I wish a girl would propose to me," he pouted.

"You're gay," I said.

"Aren't you too?"

"No! I mean, well, I'm bisexual. That's why I never talk about it on my channel. Everyone just assumes that I'm gay and I have some friends who think the bisexual thing is just a cover. But it's not. So I choose not to discuss it at all. It's not hard for you, being out on your channel?" I asked.

"I mean, there will always be asshole commenters, but I couldn't care less about them. I'm happy with who I am. I don't want to hide that."

I stood up and the room swam out of focus. "Whoa, I think I drank too much." I ran to the bathroom and gulped down three huge glasses of water. When I got back into the room, I was stumbling.

"Are you okay?" he asked, standing up.

I waved my arm as if to shoo him away. "I'm fine. I just forgot to eat dinner."

"We should get some food in you," he said.

"It's the middle of the night."

"There's an IHOP down the street. Come on. You need to eat. You look like you're about to fall over."

I let him lead me out of the hotel and to the restaurant, where we slid into a corner booth. "Scrambled eggsssss and toast, please!" I said to the waitress.

"Nothing for me, thanks," Mike said.

We flicked a wadded-up piece of napkin back and forth across the table at each other until the food arrived. I took one look at the pale yellow quivering mass on my plate and felt my stomach roil. "Ugh, no thanks," I said.

"What?" He laughed. "We *came* here because of you. Come on, you have to eat!"

I shook my head. "Not hungry anymore."

"At least have some toast."

I took a few nibbles to placate him and then slapped a few crinkled bills on the table. "Let's go back to the hotel."

When we got to the room, he flopped down on the bed, and I sat on the other side, wondering if I should lie down next to him. Even though I hadn't eaten much at the restaurant, all the water I'd guzzled and our walk through the night air had finally sobered me up.

Screw it, I thought, and stretched out beside him, making sure to inch my body closer to his so that our hands were almost touching. I glanced over at him and saw that he was looking at me. I quickly averted my eyes, and I could feel my face growing hot. It was the closest I'd ever come to being able to read someone's mind. I knew that this guy wanted to kiss me, and I couldn't believe it might actually be about to happen. He reached his arm over and started massaging the top of my head. I closed my eyes and smiled, it felt so incredible and safe. I opened my eyes and turned my head toward his. He started to lean in.

Cat suddenly burst into the room. I rolled away and sat up so fast it made my head spin. She gave me a suspicious look from the doorway. "Am I interrupting anything?"

"No, of course not," I scoffed.

"Nope," Mike said, sitting up. "Actually, I should get going. It's really late."

I glared at Cat, who just shrugged and flopped on the other bed. I couldn't blame her. We were sharing the room, after all, and it was almost dawn.

"I'll walk you to the elevator," I told Mike.

As we walked down the hallway, I wished it would start stretching out forever, like some sort of cheesy nightmare special effect from a scary movie. I didn't want him to leave. I thought for sure I was going to have my first kiss that night, and it was ending before my eyes. When we got to the elevator bank, he hit the down button and turned to me.

"Well, that was fun," he said. *Here it comes*, I thought. *My first kiss.*

And then he hugged me. That's right. A hug.

He stepped away and smiled, and before I could stop myself, I said "What, no kiss?"

He grinned and leaned in and gave me a peck on the lips. He pulled back, and then gave me another just as the elevator doors opened.

"Bye." He grinned as he got in and the doors shut.

My first thought was, *Well, that was a super-lame first kiss.* My second thought was, *Whatever. I'll take it!*

I practically skipped down the hallway back to the room. Cat took one look at the giant stupid grin on my face and asked, "Did you guys kiss?"

I threw myself face down on the bed. "Yes!"

She jumped on my bed and threw her arms around me.

"That's awesome! How does it feel?"

"Amazing. I mean, it wasn't like a *real* kiss. It was pretty innocent. But he did it twice. That still counts, right?"

"Of course it counts! When are you going to see him again?"

"I mean, soon, I hope. He has to go back to Ohio. We only have a couple of days here."

It turned out that I didn't have to wait long at all. When I woke up, Cat had already left but there was a text from Mike, asking me if I wanted to meet him in the lobby for breakfast. I felt gross and hungover, not to mention all of the butterflies in my stomach from the thought of just being near him, so I wasn't sure I could handle keeping up a conversation all by myself. I wrote back *Sure* and then immediately texted Whitney and asked her to meet us so I wouldn't have to be alone with him.

When I arrived, they were bright and awake and alert, and I felt like a total zombie next to them. They teased me about my constant groaning about how sick I felt. But the truth was that my stomach butterflies were brought on more by how strange I felt around Mike. He seemed totally fine, like nothing had happened last night, but I kept stealing glances at him and thinking, *You were my first kiss!* In the light of day, it was hard for me to fully accept, because even though I was finally able to talk about my feelings with my friends and Nicole, I was still partially removed from that part of myself.

We all split up afterward to go our separate ways, and I hugged him good-bye. "You'll be at the Maker Studios party tonight, right?" he asked.

"I have to head home and get my costume ready for the Anime Expo tomorrow," I said. "But maybe I'll stop by anyway!"

I checked out of the hotel room since I'd only booked it for two nights, and then met up with Kalel in her room so we could discuss our costumes and our plan for the next day's expo. Even though we'd never met in person, we felt like old friends from the first second.

"Ugh, I can't actually hang out right now after all," I told her. "I didn't get anywhere near enough work done on my costume. I have to go back home and work on it."

"That's silly. Just go get it and bring it to my hotel room. I'll help you finish it up!"

I knew that she was staying with her boyfriend, Anthony, from Smosh, one of the biggest channels on YouTube. It was basically the equivalent of being at Comic-Con and having Stan Lee's spouse ask you to come hang out in their room. She didn't have to offer twice.

I drove back to my apartment to pick up all of my Kid Icarus materials. The costume involved a white tunic, angel wings, gold laurel leaves for my hair, and a double-blade sword. It was pretty involved. Kalel and I worked hard all afternoon crafting the headpiece and painting the papier-mâché weapon, but the costume still wasn't complete before it was time to go to the party.

"You should just stay here tonight," Kalel offered. "We'll take the sofa cushions off and make a bed for you on the floor, and then we can finish up the costume first thing in the morning."

"You're sure Anthony won't mind?"

"Of course not!"

I thanked her, and we headed downstairs. The event was being held in the same conference room the District Lines party had been, but it was a much more formal affair. People were wearing ties, and only wine and beer were served. I spotted Mike the second I walked in, and we hugged. I introduced him to Kalel, and we all made the rounds, mingling with industry people and dancing a little, but I was still beat from the previous late night and knew I'd have to get up early for the Expo.

"You should just stay in my hotel room," Mike said, when I

told him I was thinking of going back up to Kalel's. "That way you won't have to sleep on the floor." I knew he was sharing his room with another friend, so nothing could really happen. But *because* he was sharing the room with someone else, what he was really offering was for me to sleep in the same bed as him. But Mike hardly seemed like the type to try and force himself on me in the middle of the night or anything. He was a good guy, and that was a lot of what made him attractive to me. There was nothing shady about him. He was a sweet, old-fashioned midwestern kid—the kind who probably made his mom breakfast in bed on Mother's Day.

I explained the change of plans to Kalel and promised to meet her first thing in the morning, and Mike and I headed upstairs. As soon as we got into his room, all of the exhaustion and lack of sleep from the last few days crashed down on me.

"Do you mind if I take a shower?" I asked.

"Of course not," he said. He rummaged through his suitcase on the floor and tossed me a pair of gym shorts and a tee-shirt. "Here, you can wear these to bed."

"Thanks. Ugh, I wish I had a toothbrush."

"Just use mine. I don't care. It's the blue one in the cup by the sink."

I thought that was kind of weird and gross, but I figured it was better than nothing.

When I finally got out of the bathroom, I walked out shirtless. "My turn," he said, peeling off his own shirt. My eyes nearly popped out—his abs looked as if they were cut from marble. I prayed that he'd still have his shirt off when he got out of the bathroom so I could get a second peek.

Those prayers were answered. He flicked off the lights and

crawled into bed with me. We both stared at the ceiling, our arms to our sides.

"Have you ever had a boyfriend?" he asked.

I started laughing. "Um, no. I've only ever been on one date before. And you were my first kiss."

He bolted upright. "Wait, *what*? Are you kidding?"

"Nope." I ended up explaining the whole Sam disaster to him.

"That sucks. No one should ever treat you like that," he said. He scooted back down and turned on his side so that he was facing me.

"Yeah, well, I guess I had to start somewhere," I said.

He leaned in and kissed me. Only this time it wasn't a peck. He *really* kissed me. *Ooohhhh*, I thought. *So this is what a kiss is supposed to feel like.*

Maybe I actually *should* have practiced on a cantaloupe like the Wing Girls had suggested. I had no clue what I was supposed to be doing with my tongue, and instead of just enjoying the kiss I began to get terrified that I was doing everything wrong. It was all happening so fast. Suddenly a conversation I'd had with Whitney before my disastrous date with Sam flashed through my head. We'd been talking about what to do if he kissed me.

"I had no idea what to do the first time a guy made out with me," she'd said. "It was scary, but I just sort of mimicked everything he did. I followed his moves, and it seemed to work."

So I started doing that, and she was right. Things got easier and I let myself relax and enjoy it. But after a little while, I started to get all flushed and felt like my chest was going to explode, so I pulled away.

"Are you okay?" he asked.

I could hear my heartbeat in my ears. This was all happening so fast and felt overwhelming. "Yeah," I said. "I think I just need to break for a minute." He massaged my shoulders a little, and after a while, my breathing returned to normal and we started making out again. Then it was his turn to stop and pull away.

"I really like this," he said.

"Me too."

"But I want to take things slow."

I breathed a sigh of relief. "Me too. Slow is perfect."

We ended up cuddling under the covers and falling asleep. At some point I heard his roommate stumble in and fall on the opposite bed.

Mike's alarm went off early the next morning, and I watched as he packed up his things so he could head to the airport. His friend was staying an extra day and was snoring softly on the other side of the room.

I had no idea when we'd be able to see each other next. I played it cool as we rode down to the lobby together, but inside I was obsessing over the fact that if we wanted to keep this up, it was going to have to be a long-distance thing.

We hugged good-bye and promised to Skype later that night, and then I hung out in the hotel restaurant to wait for Kalel to wake up so we could put our costumes on and leave.

Whatever, I thought, leaning back into my chair. *I can handle long distance.*

Over the next few weeks, we started a really intense Skype and text relationship. *I've been thinking*, he wrote one day. *Let's just get married and cuddle the rest of our lives away. Ok?*

Ok, awesome. Glad we had this talk.

During this time, I became painfully aware of how in love Luke and Ingrid were. I was their constant third wheel, moping while the two of them held hands and kissed everywhere we went. I wished that Mike were next to me.

After about a month of this, missing him became too much to handle, and I spontaneously decided that I wanted to buy him a plane ticket so he could come and stay with me for a week. We were both excited about the idea, but when I went to bed that night, I had trouble sleeping. Instead of thinking about all of the fun we were going to have together, I kept fast-forwarding to the moment when we'd have to say goodbye again. He had no intentions of ever leaving Ohio, and my entire life was in Los Angeles. *Is that what it's going to be like?* I wondered. *A month of agony followed by a brief bit of happiness, and then loneliness again?*

I'd been coming out to more and more of my friends, and there hadn't been a single case of someone reacting negatively. I looked at what Ingrid and Luke had, and it seemed like what they shared was something that was possible for me too. I was sick of being the odd guy out. I wanted to be able to go on double dates with them, to share what was happening in my life with an actual human in front of me instead of one trapped behind a screen thousands of miles away. The next morning I debated for hours before kicking off the following text exchange:

> **Joey:** So I've been thinking a lot about everything and I'm really not sure a visit is the best idea anymore. I obviously really like you and wish things were different but as things are now I don't see anything happening long-term! :(

He wrote back a few minutes later.

> **Mike:** Oh ok. I understand what you mean. I know for long term it's not fully the right time and of course I would never stand in your way of other relationships. I just thought you'd want to hang out and have me visit.

That broke my heart a little.

> **Joey:** I would love to hang out if you already lived here, but I just feel like a visit is a lot of attachment and that's not fair to both of us since you don't live here and nothing can actually happen.

> **Mike:** It's ok Joey. Don't feel bad. I'm just sad at the moment.

> **Joey:** It makes me sad too! I really like you but I've been thinking a lot and I just wish the distance wasn't a factor. And I know if you come and stay it's gonna be hard to say goodbye. The only time I'll see you is for short visits! And that's just not fair to either of us.

> **Mike:** I know. But at least I'm going to see you twice a year at conferences no matter what. Unless you skip out!

> **Joey:** Never! I totally still want to be your friend! And this doesn't mean something can't happen in the future! But yeah, at the moment the distance thing sucks.

> **Mike:** You better stay my friend or I will have to come visit you merely to punch you in the face. Lol. I'm sorry

if I made you feel super attached. Let me know if you
ever want me to visit as a friend Mr. Graceffa.

I felt awful. But I also knew that it was the right thing to do and
that we would remain friends. Now that I was single and had a
little bit of experience under my belt, I felt that a whole new era
of my life was opening up.

My Five Favorite Breakup Recovery Songs

1. "I'm Not Angry Anymore" by Paramore

2. "How to Be a Heartbreaker" by Marina and the Diamonds

3. "Revenge Is Sweeter" by The Veronicas

4. "In Repair" by John Mayer

5. "Potential Breakup Song" by Aly and AJ

Tips for a Perfect First Kiss

Make your first kiss count! If you are scared
and feel that you don't know what you're doing,

follow your partner's cues. This isn't the time to try out some crazy soap opera–style lip smacking. Don't psych yourself out by obsessing over the fact that it's your first kiss while it's still happening. Just go with the flow and enjoy it. Also, feel free to practice on a poster of my face. :-)

Five Celebs I'd Love to Make Out With

1. Zachary Quinto
2. Michael C. Hall
3. Spike Jonze
4. Jonathan Bennett
5. Jennifer Lawrence (just because she's Katniss. Maybe I'm a little bit bi after all!)

Chapter 17

Prince Heartbreak

Whitney could tell that I was pretty bummed out after the breakup with Mike. Even though I'd been the one to end things, it wasn't because I didn't like him; I was just trying to be a realist. What good is a boyfriend if he can never be there to experience life with you? I wanted someone to hold hands with at the movies, someone whose shoulder I could cry on when I was feeling down. And to be perfectly honest, now that I knew how awesome kissing was, I wanted a whole lot more of it in my life.

So Whitney decided to take me out in West Hollywood to see if we could find anyone. Her roommate, Colin, tagged along, and our first stop was the Abbey, one of the neighborhood's most famous gay bars. It's got gargoyles at the entrance, go-go boys inside, and Elizabeth Taylor used to pop in from time to time. Overall it's usually a blast and full of cute guys (plus a fair share of drunken whack jobs). As soon as we got drinks, we immediately met two of the latter. Their names were Edgar and Stacey.

I noticed them as soon as they walked in. Edgar had long, straight black hair and a boyish face that looked out of place on his tall, skinny body—picture a toned-down Marilyn Manson type but with Harry Styles's face. Stacey was short, with cropped auburn hair, and she was wearing a tight pair of Daisy Duke cut-offs, six-inch heels, and a black tee-shirt that was knotted on the lower hem of one side. She had tons of black mascara and eyeliner on and bright red lipstick, and there was something wonderfully trashy about the two of them that I found hilarious, so I walked right up to the girl and introduced myself.

"You're so pretty," I told Stacey after she told me their names.

Her eyes grew huge, like the Cheshire Cat in *Alice in Wonderland*. ,

"Oh, thank you, honey!" she said. "So are you! Here, I have something for you!"

She started tugging on one of her fingers until a cheap, pink plastic ring came off. She grabbed my hand and shoved it onto my finger.

"Now we're married!" she beamed.

What is it with girls wanting to marry me? I wondered, thinking back to VidCon.

"Well, lucky for you, I'm bi," I said, still keeping up the act.

She exchanged a lascivious glance with Edgar that made me think maybe it had been a dumb thing for me to say.

"Let's grab that table," Edgar said, pointing to one that had just opened up across the room.

"So what do you two do?" Whitney asked when we all sat down. I could tell that she was tolerating them only for my sake.

"I'm a screenwriter for NBC," Edgar said.

"Oh, I'm a screenwriter too!" Whitney said, relieved to have something in common. "What program do you like to use? Final Draft? Storyist? Fade In?"

"Um," he stammered. "Um, well, um, I like to just write things down, you know, on paper. I haven't really finished anything yet. Anyone ready for another round?" He practically jumped up from the table to get away from more questions. Los Angeles is filled with people like him—people who claim to be writers or actors but have never done any actual work in their entire lives. I thought it was funny, but Whitney kicked me under the table. She wasn't having any of this.

"And you?" she asked Stacey.

"I'm a hairdresser, on Melrose."

Edgar soon appeared back at the table with not just drinks but shots as well, and we all got tipsy pretty fast while chatting. The music was great, there were boys dressed only in their undies dancing on the bar, and I was feeling really happy and adventurous. Which is probably why the following happened when Whitney excused herself to go to the bathroom. I watched her make her way across the crowded room, and when I turned back to the table, Edgar had moved into her seat and was staring directly in my face. I jumped.

"Can I kiss you?" he asked.

I felt my face flush. *Oh, why the hell not?* I thought. *That is why I came here, after all.*

"Go for it," I said. I closed my eyes, expecting a soft peck on the lips, and that's just what happened—for a second. But suddenly his tongue shot out like a snake and tried to worm its way down my throat. I gagged and shoved him away from me.

"All right, that's enough," I said.

"My turn," Stacey said gleefully, and reached across the table with both hands, grabbed my head, and started making out with me. She tasted sickly sweet, like strawberry lip gloss, and I flailed my arms around with my eyes wide open. I caught poor Colin staring at us from across the table, horrified.

I managed to get her off of me just as Whitney arrived back at the table, and the tension was so thick in the air that she picked up on it immediately. "What's going on?" she asked. "What's wrong?"

My eyeballs were practically popping out of my head with the force of moving them from her face toward the door and back again, trying to signal that we needed to get the hell out of there. I tried to beam my thoughts into her head: *These people are weird, and we need to leave RIGHT NOW.*

She got the hint. "Hey Joey, Colin, let's go check out Cabo Cantina." She turned to Edgar and Stacey and said, "Maybe we'll see you guys later," before they had a chance to invite themselves along.

We rushed out, cracking up over what had just happened, and walked to the other bar, a cheesy beach-themed restaurant and lounge only a few minutes away. We got drinks, headed up to the rooftop terrace, and squeezed in at a table next to a group of other people. Immediately a cute blond guy started chatting me up, asking me my name.

"How old are you?" he asked after I told him.

"Twenty-one," I said. "You?"

"Twenty-one?" He scoffed. "You're just a baby. I'm twenty-five."

"I'm not a baby," I said, sounding, too late, exactly like a baby.

"I'm just saying that four years makes a huge difference," he said smugly. "You're basically still just out of high school."

I turned to Whitney. "Let's get out of here." I'd rather take my chances with weirdos at the Abbey than deal with a snob who spends his Friday nights at a glorified tiki lounge inflating his own sense of self-worth by insulting people younger than himself. The night wasn't exactly turning out how I'd hoped.

Back at the Abbey, it was hot and crowded, and after only one drink we decided to call it a night. I was pretty depressed. I decided I should have just stayed at home brainstorming ideas for new videos.

As we were walking out the door, I locked eyes with a guy, and the world seemed to slow down. He looked as if he had just stepped out of a Prada ad. He had soulful eyes, perfectly swept-back brown hair with a slight widow's peak, and ridiculously sharp cheekbones.

Whitney saw him, too, but we'd already left the bar. "That hot guy just totally checked you out," she said, grabbing my arm. "He's so cute!"

"I know!" I said. "What should I do? Should I go back in?"

"Maybe. You shouldn't pass someone like that up. He is sooooo sexy and clearly thought the same thing about you. Did you see the way his head turned as you walked by?"

I desperately tried to come up with a reason to walk back in without seeming obvious. Or maybe it would be a *good* thing if I seemed obvious.

I didn't have to think about it for long. He walked out of the bar with a friend and was standing a few feet away from us in the front courtyard. I got an even better look at him in the light. He was taller than he'd initially seemed and was wearing a light blue V-neck tee-shirt and jeans. He caught me checking him out, and I looked away quickly, but when I snuck a glance back he was throwing me some major eyes.

"What do I do?" I whispered to Whitney, but just then she stumbled off her heel and had to catch herself on the wall. The gorgeous guy suddenly appeared by her side and gently held her elbow to help her stand back up straight.

"You all right there?" he grinned. "A little too much to drink?"

"I'm fine, thanks," she said. "And no, I just tripped. These heels are ridiculous."

"They're cute," he said. "Hi. My name is Preston."

He was even more stunning up close, where I could get a good look at his green eyes. "I'm Whitney," she said. "And these are my friends Joey and Colin."

He looked at me and smiled, and I couldn't think of a single thing to say. "What do you do?" I blurted out. It was such a lame first question, but it was all I could think of.

"I'm a model, and I just moved out here a month ago from Illinois to pursue acting."

Him and everyone else in this town, but he made it sound charming, and he was good looking enough to actually make it happen. "What about you?"

"He makes YouTube videos," Whitney cut in. I could tell she was trying to pump me up in his eyes. "He just posted a new one today and it already has over 100,000 views."

"Yeah? I want to see!" He pulled out his phone. "How do you spell your name?"

I told him and watched as he Googled me. The new video was a cover of "We Are Never Getting Back Together" by Taylor Swift that I'd recorded with Luke, and it featured us fighting over a girl, but at the end, we walk off together and I grab Luke's butt. It's not very subtle.

I watched Preston's face as he watched it, and he laughed at all the right places. "This is really great," he said.

"Thanks. That's cool you're an actor. I want to get more into that," I said.

"You should try this one acting class that I just started going to. The teacher is phenomenal. I've already learned so much."

"That would be awesome," I said, but felt my heart sink as I saw Edgar and Stacey come stumbling out of the bar. I tried to duck behind Preston so they wouldn't see me but it was too late.

"Jooooeeeeyyy!" Stacey screeched and ran over to my side with Edgar right behind her.

"You returned," he said, rubbing my back while Stacey put her arm around my shoulder. "We missed you!!"

They were tanked and could barely stand up. "I, uh, yeah."

"Who's this?" Edgar asked, looking Preston up and down and licking his lips. I wanted to die. *Go away go away go away*, I silently pleaded. They were going to ruin everything.

Preston ignored him and looked at me as I squirmed away from their fondling grips. "Are these friends of yours?" he asked.

"We're marrrieeed!" Stacey cackled.

"I just met them tonight. I have no idea who they are," I said.

"He's coming home with us," Edgar said.

"Um, no, I am not," I said.

"Come on," Stacey pleaded and grabbed hard at my arm again. I tried to struggle free.

"Hey, why don't you guys piss off," Preston said. "He obviously doesn't want to talk to you."

I think I fell in love right there and then. He was fighting for me! God, it was hot.

"Asshole," Edgar muttered. "Come on, Stacey. Let's go. We know when we're not wanted."

"Must happen a lot," Preston called after them, and I cracked up.

"Thanks. You really saved me. They were all over me at the beginning of the night. We actually left earlier because of them."

At this point Whitney had turned to Colin and was

pretending to talk to him to give us our space, but I could tell she was hanging on to every word.

"So listen," he continued. "I've got to get my friend Alex home. He's a little drunk." He pointed to the guy he'd been standing with inside, who waved at us. "But let me see your phone. I'll put in the name of that acting studio so you can check it out."

"Sure," I said, handing it over while desperately trying to think of something to make him stay, but before I could come up with anything, he handed my phone back and then he was gone. I looked at what he had entered and saw that he had included his own number along with the studio information.

"Oh my god, Joey, that guy is SO HOT," Whitney said as we walked to the car.

"I know. He put his number in my phone."

"You have to text him!"

"Already? That's crazy."

"No it's not. Screw it. You should jump on this. And then you should jump on *him*."

I laughed as I climbed into the backseat. "He even wrote his last name. Prince. Preston Prince. I wonder if that's his real name. It sounds made up." I quickly typed out a brief text: *Nice to meet you Mr. Prince.* I hit Send while I still had the courage.

I must have checked my phone over a hundred times by the time he wrote back the following day: *When do I get to see you next?*

I breathed a huge sigh of relief that he'd written back. It felt like I'd been holding my breath all day. My fingers shook with nervous excitement as I typed out my answer.

I don't know, when are you free? So much for playing it cool.

Tonight. Want to go out? I felt a ripple of excitement run through my whole body.

Sure.

I jumped up and down on my bed while I called Whitney. "He wants to go out! Where should we go?"

"I went to this place called Saddle Ranch recently. It's kind of country western kitsch," she said. "It was fun, and it's a good first date place. Not too serious, and the decor is sort of ridiculous so there's a lot to laugh at. I think there's even a mechanical bull."

I suggested it, and Preston was game. But then things kept coming up. He had to move the time back an hour, then another hour, and then finally he asked if we could reschedule for the following day. I started to get nervous that he was going to blow me off, but he was apologetic and promised that we'd have a great time.

The next morning I surveyed my closet and pulled out five outfits, placing them on the bed. I mixed and matched the shirts and pants and shoes all along the floor, trying to find the perfect combination, before deciding to play it safe with skinny jeans and a gray-and-green-striped tee-shirt. I left the house early to give myself plenty of time, but in LA, that doesn't always help. I got on the 405 and almost immediately found myself stuck in gridlock. I cursed myself for not checking the traffic, and up ahead I could see fire billowing out of a horrible multiple car wreck. I was terrified for the people involved but still took a couple of photos on my phone to show Preston in case he didn't believe me about why I was late. *See?* I imagined myself saying. *I wasn't here on time because a bunch of people got killed.* I realized how morbid and callous that sounded and deleted the pictures.

As I finally reached the exit, I got a text from him. *I'm here.*
Running just a little late, I wrote at a red light. *Ten more
minutes!*

It was more like twenty by the time I found parking and
reached the restaurant. The outside of it looked like a Disney
ride, with cowboy and saloon girl mannequins standing in the
upper windows. It was sort of creepy, like a whorehouse version of the Pirates of the Caribbean ride.

I was just about to open the door when he called my phone.
"Hi," he said. "I'm here at the door."

"Me too. I'm so sorry I was late."

"Wait. I don't see you."

"I'm in front of the door."

"Is this some kind of a joke? I'm right here, and you aren't."

For a second, I freaked out, wondering if there was more
than one location and I'd gone to the wrong one.

"I'm facing Sunset, and I don't see you anywhere," he
continued.

I relaxed. I was at the door next to the parking lot, so I
jogged around to the other side of the building.

"Here I am!"

He smiled, showing off his perfect teeth. I pictured a little
white star twinkling on them for a second, like in a toothpaste
commercial.

"I thought you were ditching me," he said as he gave me
a hug hello. He was wearing some sort of deliciously crisp
woodsy cologne.

Never, I thought. "I got stuck in traffic. There was an awful
accident."

We sat down at a table and I grinned nervously as the

waitress gave us menus. Preston waved his away. "I already ate," he told her. "Can I just get a Ranch AMF?"

"Sure thing. And you?"

"You're not eating?" I asked him. "I'm starving!"

He gave me a funny look. "I thought we were just meeting for drinks. I ate before I came."

Damn. I didn't want to be the only one of us eating any-thing, but I was going to have a blood sugar meltdown if I didn't. "I'll just have that," I said, pointing to some sort of chicken and vegetable special they had. "Sorry," I said after she left. "I spaced on the eating part."

"You don't have to apologize for wanting to eat," he laughed. "So where'd you find this place?"

"My friend Whitney suggested it. You met her the other night."

"Right. So are you going to ride the bull?" he asked, nod-ding at the corner where a drunken girl was screaming wildly before being tossed head first onto the cushioned flooring that surrounded the machine.

I shuddered. "I don't think so. I like my neck. I don't want to break it."

The waitress came back with his drink. It was an alarm-ing shade of blue, like antifreeze. "Here's your Ranch AMF," she said.

"Oh yeah, I forgot," he said. "It said on the menu that I should ask you what AMF stands for."

"'Adios, Mother Fucker,' " she said. "Your food will be right out."

We both laughed. He took a tentative sip and then pushed it toward me. "I think we should probably share this. The menu said it has vodka, rum, gin, and tequila in it. I don't know what I was thinking."

We took turns taking small sips until my food arrived. He must have been hungrier than he thought because he ended up eating most of my food. I was still starving but far too nervous to eat. But after a while, I started to calm down. He was easy to talk to. We discussed everything. I told him all about my life in Massachusetts and how I got started doing YouTube. He told me about growing up without much money in Illinois and then escaping to college in the Northeast before deciding to try his luck in California.

I felt a little surge of pride every time I saw someone at another table check him out. It's hard not to notice someone as good looking as he is, and every time I caught someone staring, guys and girls alike, I thought: *Back off; he's with me.*

Before I knew it, almost five hours had passed and he had to leave. I quickly grabbed the check before he could make a move for it (I'd learned my lesson).

Outside, we hugged good-bye, and as I stepped back he said, "Smile if you want to hang out again."

I grinned.

"I'm going to Musical Monday at Eleven Bar tomorrow with a bunch of friends. Why don't you come with us?"

"What's Musical Monday?"

"People sing show tunes and stuff. It's actually really fun. You should bring Whitney."

If he was ready to introduce me to his friends, I knew the date must have gone well.

"I'll see you tomorrow then."

I called Whitney as soon as I got home. "It was amazing," I

told her. "You have to come to this thing with me tomorrow so we can meet his friends!"

"I have plans," she said. "And I can't get out of them. I'm sorry. You should bring someone else!"

But I didn't want to invite anyone else. In truth I was a little relieved she couldn't make it, because that meant I'd be alone at the end of the night, which would make it easier for us to possibly go off by ourselves.

When I arrived at the club the next evening, I did a quick scan of the room but didn't see him anywhere. The place seemed huge—with a balcony and tons of banquettes—and it was packed. I started to feel a little claustrophobic so I went in search of the bathroom. It's something I like to do anytime I go somewhere new—immediately find the bathroom, because it's usually quiet and it gives me a second to calm down and get my bearings. Plus I always have to pee when I'm nervous. I got a text from Preston while I was in there.

Where'd you go? I just saw you!

Bathroom. I'll be right out.

He was waiting for me outside the door and gave me a hug. "Come on," he said. "I want you to meet all my friends. We have a booth."

We got to the table, and I felt dizzy. There were at least six people sitting with him, and they all looked cool and so-phisticated. I felt like a child next to them, but they were all very friendly. Preston must have already told them a little bit about me because they started asking me all about YouTube stuff.

This one guy named Jake who was sitting across from the table seemed particularly interested.

209

"So how did you get started?" he asked, leaning in. I felt his knee brush mine under the table, and I jerked back.

I started to tell him the whole story of WinterSpringPro, but all I could think was, *Is this guy hitting on me?* I was obviously there as Preston's date. At least *I* thought it was obvious. Had Preston told these people that I was just a friend, or was this other guy being totally sleazy? I snuck a glance at Preston, and he was deep in conversation with one of the girls at the table and I felt a twinge of confusion. I turned back to Jake and continued to talk to him. He stared directly in my eyes the whole time. At least *someone* was flirting with me.

It was hard to hear people over the sound of the performers onstage who were singing Broadway hits. Preston even jumped up at one point and sang some campy song about how everything was coming up roses. He had an okay voice.

After that, his friends kept getting up to leave one by one, until finally it was down to Preston and Jake and me. Preston seemed oblivious to the fact that Jake had been hitting on me, and suddenly I had a terrifying thought. *What if this is all some ploy for a three-way?* There was no way in hell that was going to happen. But now that the thought was in my head, I couldn't get it out. What if Preston was actually some sort of horrible creepy monster? What if they had roofied my drink? It occurred to me that I didn't really know this guy at all.

Preston finally said we should go, and I warily followed the two of them out to the parking lot, where Jake finally, thankfully, said good-bye and left.

"Do you mind giving me a ride to my car?" Preston asked. "I parked kind of far away."

My heart sank as I remembered the time Sam had said

those words to me when he ditched me on our date. *I know how this ends,* I thought.

But he wasn't acting like he was trying to ditch me. In fact, when we got to his car, we ended up sitting and talking for twenty minutes about dumb stuff like the weather. I eventually turned the engine off so I wasn't wasting gas, and the sudden silence ramped up the tension. I wanted to kiss him, but I couldn't. He was too beautiful. And since he was older, it seemed like he should make the first move. I was pretty sure that he wanted to kiss me too but was holding back. Then suddenly he just said, "Okay, well, I'd better get going," and hopped out of the car.

I cursed myself for not having the courage to go for it. I worried that I'd blown it and I'd never hear from him again, but he texted later that night saying how much fun he'd had, and so I relaxed.

I wanted to see him again as soon as possible, but he always had some sort of casting or acting class that he needed to go to.

All of these auditions make me feel like such a whore sometimes, he texted me one day.

You'd probably make more money working the streets, I wrote back.

Seriously.

Well let me know when you go that route. I'll come by for a visit.

Lol I'll have to give you some sort of special offer.

Whoa. He took that and ran with it. I felt myself blush.

You have to kiss me first.

Don't worry, I will.

He asked me on a third date for the following week—drinks at Pink Taco, a disturbingly named Mexican restaurant. I was determined to kiss him this time, no matter what happened. We'd pretty much set it up as a certainty based on that last text exchange. I met him at the bar and we were laughing and catching up when suddenly we heard someone say, "Hey, Preston!"

We turned around and I recognized the guy as his friend from the night we first met at the Abbey. "Hey Alex," Preston said. "What are you doing here?" He seemed annoyed.

"You said you were gonna be here!"

"Yeah, with Joey."

"Well, I figured I'd come by," he said and then squeezed between us and ordered a margarita.

Sorry, Preston mouthed. I just shrugged. It was annoying, but having someone else around did make conversation a little easier. It took the pressure off.

After a while Alex got a text and told Preston that their friend Gwen was hanging out down the street at Cabo Cantina and that we should go meet her there. Preston raised an eyebrow at me.

"Sure," I sighed. Might as well add a fourth person to our date. It's not like we had any privacy anyway.

When we got to the cantina, I recognized Gwen as one of Preston's friends from the Musical Monday night. We grabbed a table and chatted for a bit before Preston got up to use the bathroom. As soon as he left, Gwen turned to me.

"I just want you to know that we—all of Preston's friends—really like you."

"Aw, that's sweet," I said. "I really like all of you guys too!"

"In fact, we think you're perfect for him."

"That's awesome. I like him a lot, and I've really loved getting to know him so far."

"Well, there's one thing you should probably get to know about him sooner rather than later."

"Yeah? What's that?"

"Preston is . . ." She exchanged a quick glance with Alex, who nodded in support. "He's a very complicated boy."

What the hell does that mean? I thought. I wanted to ask her questions but I didn't have time. Preston was already striding back to our table. "I can handle complicated," I told her with as much confidence as I could muster. I didn't want to show any sort of hesitation. I wanted to prove to these people that I was strong and an adult and could tackle anything thrown my way. Still, it was a *really* weird and vague thing for her to say. "Complicated" could mean practically anything. (Worse, I suddenly got the Avril Lavigne song stuck in my head.)

Preston had to be up early in the morning for yet another audition, so we ended the night and left his friends at the bar. I drove him back to his car, and he spent the ride slowly emptying an entire container of Sour Ice Breakers into his mouth. When I found his car, I pulled up alongside it and put on my hazards.

"So," I said.

"You really like these things, don't you," he said, rattling the can of breath mints. "You always have them in your car."

"You're the one eating them all," I said.

I heard him start crunching up the one that was currently in his mouth and quickly swallow it, like he was preparing. *Does this mean it's time to kiss?* I wondered. Forget butterflies in my stomach—I was so nervous that I had a whole freaking butterfly sanctuary inside me. We *had* to kiss! I wasn't going to take no as an option. I glanced at him out of the corner of my eye and he was staring at me. I looked away quickly and heard him laugh, so I slowly turned my head back to him. Even though it was dark, I could still see little flecks of light from the streetlights dancing in his emerald eyes. I leaned in, he leaned in, and we finally kissed.

I was better at it this time. At least that's what I think looking back on it, because while it was happening I was incapable of any coherent thought at all. There was no anxiety about the fact that I was making out so heavily with a guy—it felt completely natural. It was everything you want a kiss to be—his lips were crazy soft and he gently cupped the back of my head with his hands. When we finally finished making out, I realized almost thirty minutes had passed.

"Wow," I said. "I like you."

"I like you too," he smiled. He gave me another quick kiss and jumped out of the car.

He texted me later that night: *I really like kissing you.* This guy was a charmer. He knew exactly what to say to make me feel special, and it's what made me start to fall hard for him. I felt like I was floating for the next few days. I kept reliving the night in my head over and over, and I'm sure Whitney and Cat and Luke all got sick of me constantly talking about it. I couldn't wait to see him again and told him as much, but once again he got really busy with auditions.

One day when I checked in to see what he was up to, he said he was recording an audition for a primetime teen drama.

I can't get the lighting right in my room for my webcam, he texted. I immediately called him up.

"You're using your *webcam* for a big audition?" I said. "That's crazy. You need to present yourself like a professional if you want to be taken seriously."

"It's all I've got."

"Why don't you come over and let me record you? I've got a really great camera and a whole lighting setup that I use for my videos."

"You'd do that?"

As long as you make out with me afterward, I thought. "Of course!"

I scrambled to clean my room, and by the time he arrived, I had the camera equipment all set up. He was wearing a pale green deep V-neck tee-shirt and the forest-like cologne I loved. We made out for a little while before getting started.

"Come on," he said with a laugh as he finally rolled away. "We should get moving."

I made him stand in one spot until I got the lighting just right, and then we filmed several takes of his audition. In the scene, he played a high school kid who was breaking up with his girlfriend, and he had to be serious and sad. He played it a few different ways (sad, sadder, and saddest) and then we watched the videos and chose the best one (we decided on the midrange version).

He flopped down on my bed and patted the area next to him. I crawled into his arms, and we made out some more.

"Thank you so much for letting me use your stuff," he said. "I feel really good about this audition."

He changed his mind the next day, though.

After watching it again, I feel like it's all wrong, he texted. *Can I come back over and redo it?*

So he came back over and we reshot the scene. I couldn't really tell the difference between the two performances, but he seemed happier, and we got to make out some more. At one point, I pulled away.

"I'd really love for you to meet my friends," I said. "I've already met so many of yours, and I think you'd get along with mine."

"Sure," he said, but he seemed hesitant. It was the first red flag I had about him. He had no problem with me meeting all of his friends, but he wasn't interested in mine? Maybe this is what Gwen meant when she told me he was complicated. (Cue Avril.)

I pushed the thought out of my head, though, and planned a beach day in Santa Monica with Whitney and Luke and Preston. I even went out and bought a new bathing suit for the occasion, but the morning of the date, Preston canceled.

Really sorry, he texted. *A casting came up and it's super important. You guys go on without me.*

But the whole point of the day was for him to meet everyone. I grew depressed and called off the whole thing. I didn't feel like going to the beach anymore. I also lied to Luke and Whitney and said that Preston had gotten sick. I didn't want them to have a bad impression of him, but not telling them the truth also meant that I had no one to commiserate with.

I texted him later that afternoon to see how the casting went, but I didn't hear back from him until the next day. That's when I knew I was in trouble. I had fallen hard for a guy who was pulling away before anything had even really had a chance to start.

When he finally did answer me, I decided to be direct. *I have to be honest*, I texted. *I was worried that you had canceled because you had lost interest in me.*

If I had, I'd tell you, he wrote. And then I didn't hear from him again for another two days.

In retrospect, it seems pretty classic. Everyone has that first time that they fall for the wrong guy and get hurt. The difference is that most people experience that for the first time at a fairly young age, so by the time they're in their early twenties, they have a set of coping mechanisms to help them deal if it happens again. But I was operating with nothing. I had zero experience, and so when it came to Preston, I felt like one big exposed raw nerve. He'd still text with me, but it would take hours and hours for him to answer even a simple little hello or question. And during those hours, I'd drive myself insane, imagining all sorts of scenarios of him making out or even sleeping with other guys. I'd work myself up into a total frenzy until I'd finally hear back from him, and he'd have some excuse, like he'd left his phone at home or its battery had died.

After a couple of days of my barely holding it together, he finally asked if I wanted to come over to his house and hang out. I felt a massive flood of relief. If he wanted me to visit, I reasoned, then he must really have feelings for me.

He lived up in the Hollywood Hills, and I had to park on a winding road near a gate that guarded his driveway and then call his cell so he could let me in. He rented the guest cottage of someone else's house, so he didn't have a proper front door. It was like he was barricaded in some fortress. It wasn't the kind of home you could just show up at unannounced. You had to be expressly invited.

He met me at the gate, and we walked to his little studio behind the main house. It was sparsely decorated—just a bed, couch, coffee table, and a half-empty bookshelf. The kitchen was basically in the same room as his bedroom and living room. The whole house was strangely boring and vanilla, except for a Jacuzzi out back. No personal flourishes marked the space as his own—basically the exact opposite of how I like to live.

We talked a lot that night. I opened up to him about my relationship with my mom, and later he suggested we go for a hike up in the hills. I filled him in more about my life as we wandered around, finally ending up at a lookout point with a stunning view of Los Angeles. We were both silent, taking in all of the lights below us, when suddenly a bunch of red and blue ones started flashing behind.

A police car had pulled up, and the officer informed us that this particular lookout point was closed after dark.

"Sorry, we didn't know," I started to say, but the cop interrupted me. "Sit down on the curb, both of you."

I was terrified and did what I was told. Preston sat down too, but he was much calmer. "Officer, we're sorry. We were just on a walk and didn't realize how late it had gotten." His voice sounded so innocent.

"I'm still going to have to give you a ticket," the cop said.

"Is that really necessary? We were just taking in the view. I mean, how beautiful is that?" He gestured to the vista behind us and flashed the cop a huge smile, showing off all of his gleaming white teeth.

The cop gazed over our shoulders, and then back down at Preston. "Well, all right," he grumbled. "Get on out of here. And remember that these lookout points are off limits once the sun sets."

We scurried down the hill and back to Preston's house, cracking up the whole way. The fact that he had just charmed our way out of a fine made him seem even hotter to me than before.

When we got back to his house, we started making out on

his bed and cuddling. All of my frustration about him ditching my friends dissolved. *It was just a casting*, I told myself. We all came to LA to succeed, and you have to be driven in order to do that. I told myself that he was just being dedicated to his craft. And now that we were hanging out again and having so much fun, I was becoming more hopeful.

"I like having you in my bed," he said after pulling away for a moment. "You're good at cuddling."

"Thanks. I like being in your bed too," I said.

He rolled on top of me and started kissing my neck. I had no idea anything could feel so amazing.

After a couple of hours, I finally got up to leave. I wasn't ready to sleep over yet. Although I felt better about things between us, I knew that I needed to wait a while before sex came into the picture. It might seem old-fashioned, but it's a really big deal to me. I didn't want to waste my first time on someone who wasn't head over heels in love with me.

"So when do you want to hang out again?" he asked as I put on my shoes.

"Tomorrow?"

He laughed. "Wow, someone's eager."

I shrugged. "I like hanging out with you."

"Well, I have an acting class tomorrow, but I could probably do Tuesday."

And that's basically how the whole relationship operated from there on out. We'd see each other every few days, and I'd wait in agony for him to return texts on the days we didn't see each other. My attraction to him was about more than just his good looks. Preston's lack of communication fed a curiosity in me that, looking back, was pretty unhealthy. His refusal to open up and fully let me into his world just made me want him more. He was a mystery I desperately wanted to crack. His aloofness made him seem especially cool, and I wanted to be a part of that world. It's classic, really. The heart tends to want exactly what it can't have.

Whitney was at my house one night when he came over, and she decided that she didn't like him. "I don't know. There's just something a little off about the way he acts," she told me after he'd left. "It's as if he isn't really there. And wasn't he also wearing a deep V-neck tee-shirt that first time we met him at the Abbey? He likes his chest an awful lot."

"He has a nice chest," I said defensively, but she was right. If he wasn't wearing a revealing tee, he wore a button-down shirt with the top three buttons undone. Whitney started calling him Deep V from then on. *How's Deep V treating you? You seeing Deep V tonight? Joey and Deep V sitting in a tree* . . .

Over the next few weeks, our make-out sessions went further and further, but I still wasn't ready to go all the way with him. It was torture, but I knew that the trust had to be 100 percent there, and it wasn't. It's not that things were bad, but he still seemed to be keeping me at arm's length, making me wait hours before ever returning a text or phone call.

I knew that his birthday was coming up, and that gave me some hope. Birthdays are milestones, and special days are supposed to be spent with the people you love and care about. I couldn't wait to find out if I was going to be included in anything he had planned. But he never brought it up, and so on the actual day, I texted him a happy birthday message and asked if he had any plans.

Thanks, he wrote. *I don't think I'm going to do anything, but I'll let you know if I do.*

I didn't hear from him for the rest of the day or night. When I texted him the following day to see how his birthday had been, I had to wait the usual three hours before getting a response. *I was tired. I just ended up getting a drink with Alex at a bar and then going home early*, he wrote.

Can I take you out for dinner tomorrow to celebrate? I asked. He agreed, but I was still hurt.

"He could have asked me to meet them out," I moaned to Whitney. "He really doesn't like me."

"Who cares what Deep V thinks?" she said. "You can do better. Let's go out tonight. You can flirt with some guys. It'll make you feel better."

So we went to the Abbey but I wasn't really feeling it. (At least Edgar and Stacey weren't there.) We eventually ran into an actor we knew named Tim and started chatting with him. While catching up, he mentioned that he'd recently gone on a casting for a pretty big show on Fox.

"Oh, I heard about that," I said. "My friend Preston went to that too, but he didn't get it."

"You know Preston?" Tim asked, surprised. "How funny. I was just at his house last night."

I felt this weird adrenaline feeling shiver through me, and it was hard to even hear myself think due to the rushing sound in my ears. The noises of the bar seemed to recede.

"Wait. What?"

"Yeah, it was his birthday. He had a party."

"Excuse us," I said, and dragged Whitney away. "What the hell?" I said once we were safely in a corner. "Why didn't he invite me? He lied to me!"

"You need to have an actual talk with him about you two,"

she said. "You've been dating for almost two months but he's keeping you at bay. You need to know if he is seeing other people."

"That's such an awkward thing to ask," I groaned.

"But you have to!" she said. "Joey, you could get really hurt by this guy. You need to know what his deal is, and the sooner the better, so you can decide if you can handle dating him."

"I can't believe I told him I'd take him out to dinner."

"You're too nice to him. Promise me you'll clear things up with him tomorrow. Find out once and for all if you guys are even really together, or if it's just a casual hook-up thing."

I'd made a reservation at Maggio's, an Italian restaurant at The Grove. He texted me to meet him on the bridge there, and when I approached him, the whole scene felt straight out of a Disney movie. He was alone on the bridge, and there were sprays of water from fountains bubbling up all around him in the background. He was wearing the usual unbuttoned shirt, but I didn't care. I was just happy to see him. We hugged hello before sitting down, but Preston was already acting distant. He was fidgeting with his napkin and kept glancing around the room. I wanted to acknowledge right off the bat that I knew he'd lied to me.

"So, I went to the Abbey last night," I started.

"Yeah? Did you meet anyone?"

That wasn't what I was expecting at all. He said it in a way that obviously meant he was asking if I'd hooked up with anyone. And it was mischievous, as if he wouldn't have cared at all if I had.

I plowed on anyway. "I ran into Tim. He said he went to a birthday party at your place."

Preston didn't even blink. "Oh yeah, after we went to the

bar, Alex invited him back to my place for a nightcap. It was hardly a party."

His answer was too slick, but I was relieved that he didn't try to outright deny it.

"How come you didn't invite me?" I asked.

"It was late, and they were only over for, like, half an hour. Seriously, it was no big deal."

I didn't have any choice except to believe him, and I couldn't bring myself to just ask him if he was seeing other people. The rest of the dinner conversation was stilted and awkward, but at least we ended up making out in my car at the end of the night, which gave me hope that things were still good. The next few days were filled with the usual texts followed by long silences, though, and I was in absolute agony. So I was caught off guard when he ended up inviting me over to his house a week later.

"Sure, but is it okay if I come by in about an hour?" I asked. "I have to finish filming a video for tomorrow's post, but it shouldn't take long at all."

"No problem. I'll see you in a little bit," he said.

But finishing the shoot took a lot longer than expected, and then I got stuck in horrendous traffic trying to get to his place, so by the time I arrived, it was over two hours later.

I parked near his gate and texted him. *I'm here!*

Ten minutes went by.

Sorry, I'm so late, traffic was awful.

Still nothing.

I called his cell, but it went to voice mail. I sat in my car, wondering what to do. Almost half an hour passed and I was getting ready to just give up and drive home when he finally called.

"Nice of you to show up," he said in a cold tone.

"I'm so, so sorry, it was the traffic."

"It's fine," he sighed. "I'll be right down." It was like he was doing me the biggest favor in the world.

A few minutes later, he unlocked the gate and led me to his studio. I tried to apologize again, but he just sort of waved his hand at me.

"Do you want some sangria?" he asked once we got inside.

"Sure," I said. He poured us each a glass and sat down on the bed near me. I kept trying to make small talk, but there was too much awkward tension in the air. Finally he just blurted out: "Do you want to go in the Jacuzzi?"

"Okay," I said, and he tossed me a bathing suit. We changed quickly and went outside. Once we were inside the tub, things started to relax between us. He glided through the water so he was sitting next to me and we started kissing. But things got too steamy—literally, there was too much steam coming out of the water and it got really hot—so we went back inside.

We crawled into bed and he said, "This is fun."

But instead of agreeing, I was finally calm enough to just say what was really on my mind. "What exactly is this, though?" I asked. "What are we doing?"

"What do you mean?"

"Are you seeing other people? I just need to know. I can't go any further with you if you're seeing anyone else. I need to protect myself."

He sighed and rolled onto his back, staring at the ceiling. I watched his profile, holding my breath.

"I just moved here," he said. "And it was for my career. I don't want to get into a relationship yet."

"I don't want us to see other people," I told him, trying to hold it together.

"I can't make that commitment," he said.

I knew in my heart that was what his answer was going to be, but it still stung. I rolled over onto my back and peered at the ceiling too, trying to figure out what he was focusing on up there.

"What are you looking for?" he asked.

"I want a relationship with someone, and I really like you. And I'd like to know that you haven't been hooking up with anyone else this whole time." I couldn't make eye contact with him as I spoke.

He didn't say anything. I guess he didn't have to.

"Well," he finally sighed. "I guess we're not compatible."

"Is that your final decision?" I don't know why I was torturing myself like that. It was clearly over.

"I mean, things could change."

More silence.

"So are we breaking up?" he finally asked.

I leaned up on my elbow and looked at his face. He was so handsome that it actually hurt. "I don't want to, but this is really hard for me," I said. "I guess I don't have much choice." I got up and found my clothes. "I'm going to head out."

"Okay. I'll see you later. I guess."

"Of course, we will," I said. "I mean, we're going to stay in touch, right?"

"Yeah," he mumbled in a way that I knew really meant *not so much.* He got out of bed and walked me to the door, where we kissed one last time before I left.

I was fine the first day. Whitney came over and helped boost my self-confidence by continuously making fun of Deep V. *I can find someone else*, I thought. *Someone better, who actually wants a relationship. I deserve to be treated better.*

I crashed twenty-four hours later, though. Preston never got back in touch, and I thought about him nearly every day. I kept an eye out for him every time I went out to the bars, but it was as if he had disappeared from the face of the earth. I wondered if he moved back home. It took all of my strength to not call or text him, despite being desperate for some sort of closure. I wanted at least to know that we could still be friends or to be able to see him in a different light, one that didn't shine up at him on a pedestal. Because despite how he treated me, I still thought he was the perfect guy. I figured that if he didn't want me, then there must be something wrong with me.

The breakup fed into a secret insecurity that I usually kept pretty buried—that I was just some random kid from Massachusetts who didn't deserve to be in Los Angeles; didn't have what it takes to really make it (even though in reality I was doing pretty great). The fact that he could handle sleeping with other people and I couldn't made me wonder if I was being naive about what it means to date people. Maybe I needed to be less sensitive and toughen up.

But that's not who I am. I believe in love and being exclusive with someone you're intimate with. I wanted to hold on to those beliefs.

Eventually I moved on. I even casually dated a couple of other guys, but nothing serious. Preston haunted the back of my mind, and I secretly compared every guy I met to him. But things got a little easier every day, especially once I got the opportunity to embark on the adventure of a lifetime.

Favorite Love Songs of All Time

"Young and Beautiful" by Lana Del Rey

"Still into You" by Paramore

"Numb" by Marina and the Diamonds

"Time to Dance" by Panic! At the Disco

"This Is How It Feels" by the Veronicas

Top Five Sappy Movies

Any time that I feel like I need a good cry or a reminder that love really does exist, I just watch one of these tearjerkers.

A Walk to Remember

Stepmom

About Time

The Notebook

Twilight

How to Get over a Breakup

Get a puppy! Just kidding. Look, love hurts, and the mourning process of a breakup is different for everyone. Some people like to get right back in the game and start dating again to take their mind off of it. I think that's a bad idea. The only real cure for heartbreak is time. Distract yourself as much as possible, but also make sure to let yourself feel the sad emotions—don't bottle them up inside. Rely on your friends for support, and remember that it's okay to be vulnerable. I promise, you <u>will</u> get over the person someday. It will take time (longer for some people than others), but try to learn something new about yourself with every relationship. It will help you figure out what you really want out of a partner in the future.

Chapter 18

The Beyond-Amazing Race

You never know when your life is going to change. It was just a regular Thursday when I got a call from Cat about a crazy, exciting opportunity: "A friend of mine who's a producer just called me and said she's looking for a team of two guys to be on *The Amazing Race*. Would you be interested?" My answer: "UM, HELL YES." I desperately needed something big to distract me from the breakup with Preston, but I'd also been obsessed with that show for years. Who wouldn't want to get to travel all over the world for free while solving fun puzzles and challenges for a shot at winning $1 million? I told her Luke and I could try out together.

As soon as I got back to Los Angeles, we threw together an audition tape. On it, we talked about how Luke was a big troublemaker whenever we were together—how he would always try to get me to do dumb things like jump over a backyard fire at a party. We included a scene of us arm wrestling that we shot especially for the audition. After we sent it out, a producer named Lynne called us almost immediately and invited us to Finals Week at the Marriott in downtown LA.

We packed our bags and headed over, and from the start, it felt as if we'd been thrown into the actual Hunger Games. There were all these other teams of two on lockdown for the same reason as us, but we weren't allowed to talk to any of them. We'd see them at the pool and at the gym and during meals, but in between, everyone was hyperfocused on training for a spot on the show. When the teams did see each other, there was all this tension, like we were from different districts in Panem.

The key was learning how to nail the final interview with executives from CBS. I thought Luke and I were naturals, but after our first practice session with Lynne, she flat-out told us that we were crap.

"Listen," she said. "You can't just *tell* me that you're an adventurous person. I need to *hear* the adventure. I want the whole story, and I want details. You need to show that you can tell a good story and that you have fantastic chemistry."

We kept at it, but in the end we didn't make it. "Sorry, you're just not right for CBS," we were told. So we went home and I thought that was the end of it—until I got a phone call two days later from Lynne.

"Look," she said. "We actually really like you, but felt that the dynamic between you and Luke is just really weird. He's ten years older than you, and we think he really holds you back. Can you think of anyone else you might want to audition with?"

I thought about it for a few seconds. I could understand why they thought we might not have the best on-screen chemistry. As close as Luke and I were, I still wasn't totally used to being friends with guys. My whole life I'd always felt more comfortable around girls. So I asked if they'd be willing to consider a girl instead of a guy, and she said yes.

"Oh, well that opens a ton of doors," I said. "Let me make a call and I'll get right back to you."

I immediately thought of Meghan. Of all my female friends, she was the most adventurous and outgoing. She'd already traveled all over the world, so she would have great specific stories for the interview, and I knew she'd be awesome at navigating strange places. Plus we had a cool story about our friendship—how we had met through YouTube, and hosting channels on YouTube had become both of our full-time jobs. I figured we couldn't lose. We threw together an audition tape, dubbed ourselves Team Cute, and really amped up the charm. It worked—we got called in to do an interview in front of all the same execs. I thought we had it in the bag, but then weeks went by with no official word. Finally Lynne called.

"I have some bad news," she said. "Unfortunately we can't get you in this season, but we're going to try and keep you guys as an alternate. So if for some reason another team can't do it, you will take their place, although that's pretty unlikely at this point. You can always try again next season!"

I was bummed out. Twice now I'd put everything into getting onto the show, and twice I'd been rejected. It was Emerson all over again. To make matters worse, I had developed a serious pain in my jaw. I had known for a while that I had to get my wisdom teeth removed, and since I wasn't going to be doing any traveling, it seemed like a good time to finally get it done.

I got home from the surgery still woozy from the anesthesia and pretty high on painkillers when I got *another* call from Lynne.

"Joey, I've got incredible news," she said. "We need you to be on *The Amazing Race* after all!"

"Huh?" *You gotta be kidding me*, I thought. I wasn't sure if I was hallucinating from all the drugs.

"We had a team drop out and we need you guys!" I

Until the day we left for the race, a part of me wondered if we were going to get one last call telling us the deal was off. I just couldn't believe this was happening. We weren't allowed to tell anyone what we were doing, but I swore Cat to secrecy so that she could take over my Twitter account while I was away. I worked overtime to shoot a ton of videos for her to post on my YouTube channel so that it would seem like I was still in town.

When Meghan and I returned from filming the show, we were still under an embargo to not say anything about where we'd been, so it was a massive relief to finally get permission from the network to spill the news to everyone. Once the show started airing, we set up a weekly viewing party with Luke, Ingrid, Whitney, Cat, Justine, and whoever else happened to drop by. The tension was nuts because we were never allowed to tell anyone if we were going to get booted each week.

It was bizarre to see our experiences over the course of entire days get compressed into tiny segments. I know that reality shows are all about the editing, but I was shocked at just how much got left out. I understood why it happened, but we kept hitting Pause on the television to fill everyone in on things that didn't make the cut. Like when we were searching for our next clue on a beach in Bora Bora and found a tee-shirt tied to a branch. Meghan and I were convinced it held the information we needed, so we pored over every word on the shirt's label, until we suddenly noticed that the rest of the contestants were all digging through sandcastles on a nearby beach. Turned out the shirt just belonged to someone local who had tied it to the tree to dry.

My favorite challenge by far took place in Germany, where I was sent into an underground labyrinth to search for a clue. The only hint I was given about what I was going to experience was a note that said, "Who wants to go tripping?" I volunteered (I mean, why not?) and am happy that I did. I entered a doorway, pushed through a mirror, and descended into the most insane, hallucinogenic, *Alice in Wonderland*–style maze of tunnels. It was like being in a funhouse that went on forever, with slides to swoop down, ladders to climb, holes to crawl through, and flashing lights and creepy mannequins everywhere. By the time I reached the end—a boiler room straight out of *A Nightmare on Elm Street*—I was ready to turn right back around and explore it all over again, but I had to collect the next clue and rush to our next destination.

The hardest and worst challenge we experienced was in Switzerland, where we had to climb up a massive snowy mountain with two sleds. Once we reached the summit, we were presented with two fifty-pound wheels of cheese and each team had to take two of them back down the mountain while keeping them on our sleds the whole time. We froze our butts off, and it was almost impossible to keep the cheese wheels from sliding away.

We felt as if we were filming for months, but in reality it was only about four weeks. We finally got booted off on the tenth leg of the race. It was pretty devastating; I knew that we had much more in us. Everyone at the viewing party—including my dad, who happened to be in town visiting—got a little teary when our final episode aired. But I could hardly complain. We got to experience adventures most people only dream of. And apparently we were pretty well liked too. We ended up getting called back a year later to appear on an All-Stars edition. Never in a million, trillion years could I have imagined that the cross-country road trip I'd taken with Brittany just a few years back would have led to a much-longer journey across the entire planet.

How to Ace a Reality Television Audition Tape

1. Be an extreme version of you.

2. Have an interesting background, or make one up.

3. Share stories from your past, and <u>be detailed</u>. Relate these stories back to the show.

4. Really know the show you're auditioning for. If you notice that they keep casting certain archetypes, then play up to the one that best fits your personality.

5. That being said, put your own personal spin on that archetype. Does the show love casting a crazy, jealous bitch each season? Then be a crazy, jealous bitch who is also a cat hoarder. Let's face it, the majority of these shows are all about acting anyway.

Five Other Reality Competition Shows I'd Die to Be On (Attention, Producers!)

Survivor. After making it through so many physical challenges on <u>The Amazing Race</u>, I know I would kick ass on this show. Plus I'm excellent at making (and breaking) alliances.

America's Next Top Model. I knew how to smize before I could even talk.

Wipe Out. Even if you screw up within the first ten seconds on this show, it still looks like so much fun falling off the huge obstacle courses. But I'm pretty agile and I bet I'd make it pretty far.

Double Dare 2000. I'd need a time machine in order to do it, but I watched this show so much when I was little and I'd do anything to play. It was half crazy-easy trivia (I always knew the answers) and half challenges like digging for flags in a giant ice-cream sundae. Basically, nerd kid nirvana.

Figure It Out. Another one that isn't on anymore, but who wouldn't like to be there in person to watch celebs like Ariana Grande get slimed?

Chapter 19

The Return of Preston

It's weird how exes always pop back into your life at the worst time, just when everything is going great and you think you're finally on the other side.

I was still riding pretty high from my experience on *The Amazing Race* when I went to a NerdHQ party during Comic-Con in San Diego. NerdHQ is a big event that takes place at the same time as Comic-Con and hosts cool pop culture panels. I was standing in a corner flirting with a cute guy named Jeremy when I heard someone behind me say my name.

I slowly turned around, and there he was. Looking as gorgeous as ever and still wearing a damn deep V-neck tee-shirt. Preston's hair was a little bit shorter, but he still smelled like the same cologne I'd loved.

It was the worst timing ever. Jeremy excused himself, and Preston was grinning as if we'd just seen each other a few days ago. I saw Whitney from across the room, and she was glaring at him with death-ray laser eyes.

"What's up, man?" he said, giving me a hug. I tried to keep my arms at my sides but I couldn't help myself and hugged him back. It felt so good to be wrapped up in him again, even if for just a second. "What have you been up to? Besides *The Amazing Race,* duh. Congratulations on that, by the way!"

"Thanks. Oh, you know, YouTube stuff. It's pretty much my entire life."

"It's really good to see you," he said. "I've missed you. All this fantasy stuff has been reminding me of you today!"

He babbled on about what he was doing there, but I didn't hear a word he said. I couldn't believe he was standing there, talking to me in the flesh. I felt like I was going to pass out. I had finally, *finally* just gotten over him, and here he was again. All of my feelings for him came rushing back, and they were powerful enough to make me feel that I was having an anxiety attack. I glanced over at Whitney, and she was pointing furiously toward the door, as if to say, *Let's get out of here.*

I had no idea what to say to him so I figured she probably had the right idea. I quickly excused myself and fled.

"Holy crap," she said as we left. "What the hell is Deep V doing here?"

"I have no idea."

"Well I'm proud of you for leaving," she said. "It's better not to engage."

I knew she was right, but I lasted only about twenty-four hours before I caved and texted him.

It was good seeing you. We should have a real catch-up soon.

Totally, he wrote back almost immediately. *What are you doing next week when we're back in LA?*

I was so confused. Was he into me again? Was he asking me out on a date? I didn't know how I felt about it, so I told him I'd reach out once I got home. I didn't want to come across as too eager. When I finally did text him, his suggestion as to what we should do cracked me up. It was too ironic.

It's my birthday next week, he wrote. *I'm having a party and you should come! Bring your friends!*

I decided that he definitely wanted me back.

Since Whitney was still anti–Deep V, I brought Cat with me. The party was on the rooftop of a fancy hotel, and it was packed. I spotted Preston almost immediately, and he came bounding over and gave me a huge hug.

"I'm so glad you could come!"

I introduced him to Cat and handed him the gift I'd picked up, a bottle of Patrón. I'd almost brought him some sangria—a nod to the night we decided to end things—but decided that would be way too dramatic. "Nice," he said. "Thank you! We'll have to do a shot later." And then he winked at me.

Oh, it's so back on, I thought.

"I've got to say hi to some people, but you should get a drink! I'm sure there are some people here you remember." He disappeared into the crowd.

"What do you think?" I asked Cat.

"He did seem awfully excited to see you," she said. "But I agree with Whitney. You should be careful. Come on; let's mingle."

We grabbed drinks at the bar and hung out near the pool, eventually joining in a conversation with a small group of people standing near us.

"Timmy really went all out," a girl with platinum hair said.

"Seriously," said her friend, who looked as if she'd been hitting the lip injections a little too hard. "I can't imagine what it must have cost to rent this place out."

"Who's Timmy?" I asked.

"You don't know Timmy?" the blonde asked, laughing. "Wait, who are you?

"I'm friends with Preston, the birthday guy."

"Oh yeah," Big Lips said. "Then I'm sure you know Timmy, Preston's boyfriend."

I heard Cat gasp as my stomach dropped. I shouldn't have been surprised. I played it cool—I wasn't about to make a scene—but I managed to excuse ourselves and we hightailed it to an empty corner.

"Oh god, Joey, I'm so sorry. What a sleazy asshole. Let's get out of here."

I looked around for Preston but couldn't see him anywhere. "No. Screw it. We're at a party, and I'm not going to let his bull-shit chase us off. There are enough people here that we can avoid him." It's not like we had to try, though. I didn't see him again for the rest of the night, and despite my best efforts to meet new people and be upbeat, we eventually called it a night.

He texted the next day: *Hey sorry I didn't get a chance to talk to you more last night, it was crazy! What's your schedule like this week?*

I was starting to wonder if he was some sort of sociopath, totally devoid of empathy. I texted back that I was busy. But he kept asking, and I finally gave in about a week later when he suggested that I come over to his house. I needed closure once and for all. I wanted to just ask him outright what his deal was.

It was weird being back in his studio. Nothing much had changed, except that it looked a little smaller than I remembered. He sat on his bed, and I sat on the couch. He launched into a bunch of nervous chatter, but I interrupted him.

"So why didn't you tell me that you have a boyfriend?"

He looked uncomfortable. "I guess because I'm not really happy with him. I'm sort of confused, so it feels weird to call him my boyfriend. We started dating not long after you and I broke up."

"So that's why you just stopped talking to me last year? I thought we were at least going to stay friends."

He played with the edge of his blue bedspread, pulling at a loose thread. "I sort of stopped talking to everybody for a while after that. I was going through something. I don't know. I just wanted to focus on my career."

"How's that going?"

He shrugged, and suddenly I just felt sorry for him. The big bad wolf I'd created in my mind was gone. I'd spent over a year building him up as someone huge, almost mythological. But during that same time, I'd managed to accomplish a lot. I realized that in pushing myself to do more and more in my life and with my YouTube channel, I'd been moving on without even realizing it. I felt an enormous weight lift from my body.

I was over him.

Ten Qualities I Now Look for in a Boyfriend

1. Confidence
2. Ambition
3. Facial hair (I like them manly =P)
4. Muscles, always a plus
5. Good work ethic
6. Loving

7. Must make me laugh

8. Challenges me to be a better person

9. Makes me feel safe when I'm scared

10. Someone independent and comfortable in social settings

Six Dating Red Flags: How to Tell If He or She Isn't Right for You

1. You feel that you have to put on an act when you are around the person.

2. The person talks only about herself or himself.

3. Poor hygiene

4. You catch him or her in a lie.

5. The person doesn't challenge you to grow.

6. You sense that the person is ugly (on the inside, where it really counts).

Chapter 20

Hatorade, or That Time My Car Was Towed

The day I was cyberattacked could possibly go down as one of the worst days I had after moving to Los Angeles. Having a stampede of people come at you with all their negativity at once can seriously mess with you. It doesn't matter if you have the thickest skin in the world. That much nastiness will pierce it, and it hurts.

I had been steadily working on my own channel throughout the entire year after *The Amazing Race,* and it continued to pick up speed, but it really exploded that spring when I went to Florida for a big music and online video convention, Playlist Live. I met a couple of British YouTubers named Zoe and Louise, and we all filmed collabs with each other. They were just simple things, like playing games of Would You Rather, but it opened up my audience to a whole new country. Plus, Zoe and Louise became awesome new friends.

Within just a couple of months, I hit 1 million subscribers. I couldn't believe that so many people were interested in my life, and it was all happening so fast that I rarely had time to think about it. I just kept going. But every now and then, I'd pause and let it all sink in. The child nobody wanted to save in a health CPR class suddenly had more friends than a thousand times the number of kids in that school.

But as I learned later that fall, with great fans come great haters.

A lot of you reading this book probably know the basics about what happened when my car got towed, but I've never told my full side of the story, so here goes.

It all started on the afternoon of October 14, 2013. I had dropped off all of my tax documents with my accountant a few days earlier, and he called me to come pick up an envelope with copies of all my completed information in it. I swung by his office before heading to my friend Stacy's house to play some *Minecraft*. We had an awesome time, and later that night I headed out to go home. But my Prius wasn't where I remembered parking it. My first thought: *Oh crap, my car got stolen.*

I panicked and ran back to Stacy's and told her my car was gone. She came outside and walked around with me to look for it, since she thought I must have just parked it somewhere else and forgotten the spot.

Being a daily vlogger, I naturally whipped my camera out to share the experience. After looking everywhere, we came to the conclusion that my car must have been towed. But I had no idea why—I didn't remember seeing any No Parking signs. Stacy drove me home, and I went onto a towing website to check my license plate number. Sure enough, it had been brought in.

The next morning I had my roommate at the time drop me off at the pickup center, and after waiting for about an hour, I finally got my car back. When I asked why it had happened, the attendant told me that I had blocked someone's driveway when I parked.

That's so weird, I thought. I had no recollection of there being a driveway, and I'd never done anything like that before.

I figured my car had to have only been a little bit over the line. So once I got my car back, I vlogged about the whole thing. I was exaggerating and feeling punchy, and maybe I went a little over the line when I called the homeowner's car a fat slut who couldn't fit through the driveway if it was blocked a tiny bit. (*Obviously* it was a joke. How can a car be a slut? Fat maybe, yes, but a slut?? There's that one documentary about people trying to score a new truck called *Hands on a Hard Body*, but it's not a porno!)

Apparently, though, as I was soon to find out, calling a car a slut is considered extremely offensive. I was just ranting, as most people do when they spend a good chunk of their day doing something they don't want to do and spending good money just to get their own property back. The towing seemed ridiculous, especially because I didn't think I had done anything wrong.

I figured that was the end of the story. But it turned out that the guy who had my car towed peeked inside it first and saw my envelope full of tax documents. Not only did he learn my name, he discovered how much I owed in taxes that year because my accountant (I never went back to this one) wrote the amount on the outside of the package. I hadn't even noticed the numbers were there because they were so faint, which means that the dude had to have been seriously snooping around the contents of my car.

I learned all this because the guy was a small-time comedian. He Googled my name, watched my rant video, and decided to post his own reaction video. Shane Dawson was the first person to let me know it was out there. I opened my laptop, watched it, and cracked up when I saw that the guy had taken a photograph of my car. It was indeed blocking the

ENTIRE driveway. The whole thing was completely my fault after all!!

How the heck did I not realize that? I wondered. *I must have been really out of it that day.* I was totally embarrassed. I started to think of sheepish ways I could respond with an apology video, or maybe even leave a little "I'm sorry" gift in the guy's driveway, when suddenly he started digging in on me personally. He said that all of his friends couldn't believe that anyone bothered to watch my videos, and basically he called all YouTube vloggers dumb. He claimed that he didn't want to say anything mean about me, but then went on to throw a bunch of passive-aggressive verbal punches about things I'd said in my rant video. He even said how much I owed in taxes, and while the number was bleeped out, there are people who can read lips and it seemed borderline illegal to me.

I was stunned. The video was already going viral as I watched it for the first time, and Reddit boards were posting all sorts of nasty things about me. I started getting cruel tweets from total strangers—just a few at first, but they quickly gathered momentum until my entire feed was filled with hate. Even some news outlets were picking up the story.

It felt like I was living in an alternate reality where I'd committed some sort of incredibly taboo crime. I had no idea what to do, and so I disappeared. I stayed off the Internet as much as possible, but every time I did turn on my laptop, it felt like that scene from the first Harry Potter movie when the kids open up a forbidden book and it starts screaming at them.

Here's the thing: I've been hated on YouTube for years. It's something I got used to early on and learned to brush off. But this was different. Many YouTubers, myself included, pride themselves on how much of a community we have. Well, I certainly found out who my true friends were during that time. I was shocked to see how many YouTube vloggers enjoyed seeing me torn to shreds. It was as if they were getting high off it. I'm not going to name names, but I began to keep a list of all my fellow vloggers who trash-talked me or gave the video even more attention by posting it. Many of them sided with him and started following him on Twitter and promoting his video. They thought his irresponsible response was hysterical, and I was mortified. People who know firsthand just how painful it is to be hated on were attacking me from within my own circle.

Fortunately, my core group of friends like Cat, Whitney, Meghan, and Kalel were there for me and stood by my side. With their support, I let the dust around this dumb Internet "scandal" settle and got back to vlogging as if nothing had happened. But it taught me that I needed to put my guard up more. I closed myself off from a lot of the YouTube community and stuck with the people I already knew and trusted. And now, whenever new people enter my life, I end up questioning what their motives are—whether they are the type of person who would turn on me in an instant if it meant furthering their own agenda. It sucks, but I have to face the fact that it goes with the territory since I have chosen to live so much of my life in public. There's nothing I can do about it, so I've started to hone my skills at telling whether someone is being genuine with me. It's a good skill to have anyway, but I just think it's sad that it took thousands of strangers attacking me at once to realize it.

How to Deal with Online Haters

Here's the thing about the Internet: for every cool new person you discover on it, there's also a nasty troll ready to take you down. When Brittany and I got mean comments on our WinterSpringPro channel, they were pretty easy to ignore because the sweet messages far outweighed them.

When I started my own Joey channel, cruel comments were a little harder to take because they were directed at me specifically, not a piece of creative work that had been a joint effort. But by that time, I'd already learned how to tune out the negativity by focusing on the positive. I think the reason the whole towing thing hit me so hard was that the source of the hate came from an actual person I could see in his video instead of a commenter hiding behind a fake user name. This wasn't some faceless stranger, and his spark fueled nastiness in people I had considered friends.

The way I dealt with it was to go offline and surround myself with people I knew loved me while I gathered up my emotional strength. During that time off, I had a lot of time to reflect, and what I realized is that life is short—way too short to let strangers knock me down for doing what I love. The best advice I can give is the advice everyone gives: ignore the assholes and don't ever engage with them. But if you're being attacked online and need a little extra emotional support, here are some other things to consider:

1. Haters are just jealous.

2. You are awesome for having the courage to put yourself out there in the world.

3. If a hater is hiding behind a fake screen name, this person already knows that what he or she is doing is wrong.

4. NO ONE is universally liked.

5. I'll always support you.

Chapter 21

Looking Forward

I continued to work hard building my Joey channel, but career-wise I still felt like there was something absent from my life. I missed making movies. One day I was driving in my car and catching up with Nicole. She told me that she had randomly watched that old Nickelodeon show *Are You Afraid of the Dark?* on TV the night before and we were both laughing and trading nostalgic reactions. What a blast from the past!

But the conversation got me thinking. I was really into the show *Skins* at the time, and I started to imagine a series that was a cross between it and *Are You Afraid of the Dark?* A more adult version.

I started talking to Whitney about it, and dreamed up different characters and a plot that intertwined all of their arcs. She went off and wrote a sample script, and I loved it so much that I insisted she write all the episodes.

"Shouldn't you hire a real writer?" she asked.

"You *are* a real writer," I told her.

I decided to call the series *Storytellers*. I didn't want to half-ass this project, and I knew that in order to shoot it the way I envisioned, it would require some real money. So I began a Kickstarter campaign to try and raise $100,000. I was so excited when the drive ended because apparently we had gone beyond our goal by $40,000! How insane is that? But here's the problem with crowdsourcing, and a tip for those creative entrepreneurs among you: not everyone who pledges money has the actual cash to back it up. In reality we only brought in around $80,000, so I tried again on another crowd-funding site, Indiegogo, to make up what I still needed. The second fund-raising effort was a success, and we ended up getting $10,000 extra to spend on the show.

It was my first time producing and acting in an actual high-quality scripted short film, but because I'd been producing my own content for so long, it all came as second nature to me—except for balancing such a huge budget. I ended up having to front a lot of my own money from my savings, but it was worth it. I made it all back after we scheduled screenings in a six-city tour across America and every single one sold out within a week! We ended up adding in even more shows, and it was fun to sit in the back of the theaters and watch the audience react. I'm now trying to raise funds for a sequel, all in the hopes of continuing on the path to fulfilling my biggest dream: landing a lead role in a feature film.

I think one of the coolest things about *Storytellers* is that I got to do it my way. I was able to get an entire show made without going through all of the usual yet difficult-to-navigate Hollywood routes. I maintained artistic control of my vision, which is something people rarely get to experience in this town. I feel that I'm part of a generation that's changing the system of how we create. People are no longer slaves to the standard studio mode. If you want to make a movie or a series, there are tools out there to help you reach that goal. All you have to do is, well, do it!

Since *Storytellers*, I've shot several short films that I've either starred in or produced. I feel that I'm getting back to my childhood roots: I'm getting to make up fun tales, but now I have the resources to bring them to life in ways that are even bigger and better than I would've ever imagined. Not even a decade ago, people coming to Los Angeles could get stuck in an endless grind of auditions and jobs to make the rent, with no real creative outlet to keep them fulfilled. The Internet—YouTube, in particular—has changed all that. If you want to create, there is no one to stop you but yourself.

My Dream Acting Roles

1. Finnick in The Hunger Games

2. Thomas in The Maze Runner

3. Zane from The Uglies (if the book series ever gets made into a movie)

4. Any character on Lost

5. Any student from the Slytherin house in the Harry Potter series

How to Cry on Demand in a Movie

The classic method is to get to an incredibly sad place in your head. But if you're unable to quite go there (it can be tough with all those people and lights around!), then one thing that works for me is to start mimicking the physical act of crying. Distorting your face the way it does when you cry naturally can actually trigger your body into producing tears! It's true, I swear.

My Favorite Horror Movies

Silent Hill. I discovered this movie while flipping through channels as a kid and I couldn't look away. I didn't know it at the time, but it's based on one of the scariest video game series of all time, and watching it was like <u>being</u> in a video game—you have no idea what is going to happen next.

Insidious. The most terrifying movie about ghosts that I have ever seen. There are so many huge jump scares that still manage to make me scream every time I watch it.

Signs. I saw this M. Night Shyamalan movie with my cousin when we were little. The aliens were creepy enough as blurry, fast-moving creatures, but when we hit Pause to get a good look at one, we both ended up screaming and running from the living room. We refused to go back in.

Ginger Snaps. This is a really cool take on the werewolf genre. It's more about the relationship between two sisters, and it puts a whole meta-physical spin on all the feelings that can arise when an older sibling starts menstruating and being sexually active before the other.

The Blair Witch Project. I love the shaky-camera, found-footage aspect of this classic. Since it was all shot on video, it reminds me a lot of the style of my early movie-making attempts. It's also scary as hell.

Chapter 22

Good Damn Bye!

I guess that's it. For now, at least. I hope you've enjoyed this deep dive into my life. If this were a vlog, here's where I'd normally say, "Leave a comment down below," or "Give this a thumbs-up if you liked it!" Neither of those things makes any sense in this case, but feel free to hold the book up and give it a literal thumbs up. Actually, if you tweet me a photo of yourself doing that, I'll tweet back something nice!

Thank you, from the bottom of my heart, for continuing on this journey with me. It's funny how something as tiny as a lead paint chip launched my life into the direction it took. But I think that's always the case in life. Small things can lead to huge changes, and if those changes end up being obstacles, try to learn from them instead of letting them crush you. There were many times in my life when I thought my relationship with my mother was over, but I know it never will be. No matter how big a wall I build against her, I will always love her, even if sometimes that feels impossible. Loving an alcoholic is one of the most painful things a person can go through, and if I've been able to reach just one person who is in a similar situation to help him or her feel less alone, then this book will have all been worth it.

The same goes for closeted readers. I know that we are living in an era where it's more accepted than ever before to be gay, but that doesn't mean there aren't still people who feel ashamed or scared to act on those feelings. But it's never too late to realize who you are. It's amazing to finally be out of the closet, especially after experiencing so much pressure from online commenters to come out before I was ready to. I'm proud to be gay, but I'm even prouder that I was able to wait and reveal that part of myself on my own terms. Don't ever feel pressured into doing anything you aren't ready to do. It's always okay to be different *as long as you are staying true to yourself.* You have the power and control to become whatever you want to be, no matter where you start out in life.

I'm sure that by the time this book comes out, I'll already have a million more stories to share, and that's all because of you and the opportunities you've given me, dear viewers-turned-readers. I don't think I'll ever be able to express just how much it means to me. I love you all, and just for old time's sake, may the odds be ever in your favor.

Acknowledgments

Nicole, thank you for being the coolest older sister ever. I've always looked up to you. Mom and Bob, thanks for always loving me and believing in me, and Dad, thanks for being my number-one fan. Jett, you will always be my little squish.

To my friends: Brittany, I know we will be best friends forever—thanks for always making me laugh. Meghan, David, Cat, thank you for helping me get through the toughest of times. Mariah and Hannah—HJ for life! Thank you Saundra for your support!

Luke, thank you for making me feel okay with who I am. Pam, you're not just a trainer, you're my California mom. Hallie, I'll always be grateful for how you've helped me open my mind up and discover myself more. Jonica, we were the best of friends and I'll never forget that. And to Alison, Rachel, and Amanda, thanks for helping me survive high school!

Thank you to Joshua Lyon for helping me create this book, and to my editor, Daniella Wexler, for pushing me to get shit done. Petar Mandich, I'd be lost without you. To everyone else at Addition—your support in my life and career means so much to me. And a giant thanks to all my agents at UTA who believe in me and push me to bigger things.

Lastly, thank you to all the haters—you've only made me stronger.